Law Society of Irela...

Intellectual Property Law

Cavendish
Publishing
Limited

London • Sydney • Portland, Oregon

Law Society of Ireland

Intellectual Property Law

Editor
Dr Anne-Marie Mooney Cotter

Authors
Garrett Breen
Rosaleen Byrne
Louise Carey
Maureen Daly
Tara MacMahon
James Murray
Andrew Parkes
Ken Parkinson
Carol Plunkett

Cavendish
Publishing
Limited

London • Sydney • Portland, Oregon

First published in Great Britain 2003 by
Cavendish Publishing Limited, The Glass House,
Wharton Street, London WC1X 9PX, United Kingdom
Telephone: + 44 (0)20 7278 8000   Facsimile: + 44 (0)20 7278 8080
Email: info@cavendishpublishing.com
Website: www.cavendishpublishing.com

Published in the United States by Cavendish Publishing
c/o International Specialized Book Services,
5824 NE Hassalo Street, Portland,
Oregon 97213-3644, USA

Published in Australia by Cavendish Publishing (Australia) Pty Ltd
3/303 Barrenjoey Road, Newport, NSW 2106, Australia

© Law Society of Ireland   2003

All rights reserved. No part of this publication may be reproduced, stored in a retrieval system, or transmitted, in any form or by any means, electronic, mechanical, photocopying, recording, scanning or otherwise, without the prior permission in writing of Cavendish Publishing Limited, or as expressly permitted by law, or under the terms agreed with the appropriate reprographics rights organisation. Enquiries concerning reproduction outside the scope of the above should be sent to the Rights Department, Cavendish Publishing Limited, at the address above.

You must not circulate this book in any other binding or cover
and you must impose the same condition on any acquirer.

British Library Cataloguing in Publication Data

Intellectual property law professional practice guide
1 Intellectual property – Ireland
I Law Society of Ireland
346.4'17048

Library of Congress Cataloguing in Publication Data
Data available

ISBN 1-85941-805-8

1 3 5 7 9 10 8 6 4 2

Printed and bound in Great Britain

ABOUT THE AUTHORS

Garrett Breen qualified as a solicitor in 1994 (Law Society of Ireland). He earned a BSoc Sc (University College Dublin, 1988) and a Diploma in Legal Studies (College of Commerce Rathmines, 1990). Garrett is a partner in the Information, Communications and Regulatory Law Unit of Landwell. Prior to joining Landwell, Garrett had been with A & L Goodbody Solicitors as part of its Intellectual Property and e-Business Unit. He did his apprenticeship with Giles Kennedy & Co. Garrett advises on all aspects of intellectual property, both contentious and non-contentious. He advises in relation to copyright, trade marks, patents know-how and confidential information. In particular, Garrett has had a lot of experience in the enforcement of intellectual property rights against counterfeiters. He has been the spokesman in Ireland for the Anti-Counterfeiting Group (ACG). He has also acted for brand owners such as adidas, Reebok, Nike, Levi Straus & Co, assisting them in combating counterfeiting in Ireland. Garrett has also acted for and advised rock groups, musicians, artists, photographers, web developers and authors in relation to their ownership of copyright, the protection of it and the licensing/assignment of it. During the '.com' era, Garrett advised new '.coms' as well as established businesses in all issues relating to the building of a web presence and selling products and services on-line. This has included advice on the implications of both Irish and European e-commerce legislation as well as the legal aspects of web development, including web intellectual property.

Rosaleen Byrne is an associate solicitor in the Information and Communications Law Unit of Landwell Solicitors. Landwell is an international network of law firms with a presence in over 40 countries. In particular, Rosaleen advises clients in the technology sector in relation to e-commerce, intellectual property, data protection and telecommunications law issues. Although Rosaleen advises on all aspects of intellectual property law, she has particular experience in advising software clients in relation to the protection and exploitation of their developments. Previously Rosaleen worked in the Technology Law Unit of A & L Goodbody Solicitors and also at the Information Society Directorate of the European Commission. While at the European Commission Rosaleen was involved in the development of European legal policy on issues concerning the Information Society. Rosaleen continues her involvement with the European Commission through participating in meetings of the Legal Advisory Board to the Information Society Directorate of the Commission. Rosaleen has written a number of short articles and given numerous talks on intellectual property and technology law related matters.

Louise Carey is a solicitor at Arthur Cox. She has a Bachelors of Civil Law (BCL) (University College Cork, 1981), and a Diploma in European Law (University College Cork, 1991). She was admitted as a solicitor of the Irish Law Society in 1985, and gained entry to the Register of Trade Mark Agents in 1987. Her areas of practice include a specialism in litigation relating to all the areas of intellectual property, advisory and transactional work relating to intellectual property, and trade mark registration matters. Her knowledge of languages includes English, French and German. She is a member of the Licensing Executives Society (LES) and the Irish Trade Mark and Patent Agents Association.

Maureen Daly graduated from University College Dublin with an Honours Science Degree in Biochemistry. Prior to joining A & L Goodbody, she worked as an in-house solicitor with FR Kelly & Co, a patent and trade mark firm where she was responsible for the prosecution and opposition of Irish, community trade mark and worldwide trade mark applications. She is a qualified Registered Trade Mark Agent and Community Trade Mark Attorney and holds a Diploma in Applied European Law as well as a Diploma in Legal Studies. She advises on all aspects of intellectual property and has lectured on such matters to visiting students at Trinity College Dublin and to members of the Association of Patent and Trade Mark Agents, the Dublin Solicitors Bar Association, the Corporate and Public Services Solicitors Association, the Law Society of Ireland and First Biotech. Maureen also lectures on intellectual property to students on the BSc (Computer Science) course in Trinity College Dublin. She is also the author of numerous articles on intellectual property as well as being the Irish contributor to a book on *Character Merchandising in Europe* (the publication of which is imminent).

Tara MacMahon is an associate solicitor in the Information Technology Law Group of Matheson Ormsby Prentice solicitors (MOP). After qualifying as a solicitor in 1997, Tara worked in the Intellectual Property Department of Hammond Suddards Edge in the UK for two years, before moving to MOP. She is an Irish registered trade mark agent and has also obtained an ACCA Certified Diploma in Accounting and Finance. Tara's practice areas cover all aspects of intellectual property ownership, protection and exploitation, and related EU legal issues. Her clients cross all industry sectors, including those in the R & D, healthcare, biotechnology, information technology and branding sectors. Tara has particular experience in the area of intellectual property joint ventures and collaboration agreements, research and development agreements, intellectual property licences (both intra-group and third party) and the taking of security over intellectual property. Tara has also carried out extensive intellectual property audits for various clients. Tara is a member of the Copyright Association of Ireland (CAI), the Irish Anti-Counterfeiting Group (IACG) and the Licensing Executives Society (LES).

James Murray is a solicitor with the Commercial Litigation Department of Arthur Cox. He achieved a BA (1988) and LLB (1990) from University College Galway, and later qualified as a solicitor (admitted 1994). He subsequently obtained a LLM (First Class Hons) from the University of Cambridge (1996), including a specialism in intellectual property. He worked as a Research Associate at Cambridge 1996–97 and he has been elected a Scholar of Sidney Sussex College. Since returning to Ireland in 1998, he has specialised in Commercial Litigation, with particular emphasis on product liability, intellectual property, conflicts of law and competition law.

Andrew Parkes is a consultant to Tomkins, European Patent Attorneys and Community Trade Mark Attorneys. He is a registered patent agent in Ireland (1967) and Great Britain (1965). He is a fellow of the Chartered Institute of Patent Agents and a fellow of the Institute of Trade Mark Attorneys. He received a BA (Natural Science and Law) and MA at Cambridge University (1961, 1965). He was President of the Association of Patent and Trade Mark Agents in Ireland in 1989–91 and was also President (1990–93) and is now Honorary President of the Union of European Practitioners in Industrial Property. He was a member of the Standing Advisory Committee at the European Patent Office, SACEPO (1992–2002). He gained professional experience in England and in Washington DC (1961–68). He then returned to Ireland and joined Tomkins in 1968. He was a partner there from 1971 until 2001.

Ken Parkinson joined Whitney Moore & Keller (WMK) in 1973. He qualified as a solicitor in 1978 and became a partner in 1982. He has practised extensively in commercial litigation with a particular emphasis on intellectual property law, acting in an advisory capacity and in the conduct of litigation for both plaintiffs and defendants. Ken has also advised clients in the pharmaceutical business in relation to regulatory matters. In addition to advising many multi-national companies, Ken has been involved in many of the leading Irish intellectual property law cases such as: *House of Spring Gardens v Point Blank*, a leading case in copyright infringement and breach of confidence; patent infringement case *Wavin v Hepworth Iron Co*; and *Adidas v O'Neill* which is a leading case in passing off. He has lectured on intellectual property law both at home and abroad and has conducted courses in intellectual property law for members of the Law Society of Ireland and for trade associations. Ken is a member of the Irish Group of the International Association for the Protection of Industrial Property.

Carol Plunkett qualified as a solicitor in 1979. She practised with A & L Goodbody, and became a partner there in 1998, before joining Landwell, an international network of law firms in January 2001. Carol specialises in intellectual property, information technology, competition law and telecommunications and in particular advises on the contentious aspects of those areas. She has advised many of the world's leading brand owners as well as commercial artists regarding the protection of intellectual property rights, in the information society and in relation to the internet. She has been involved in many land mark cases on behalf of brand owners protecting their trade marks, dealing with competition matters and administrative law issues. Carol has also advised many clients in relation to privacy laws in Ireland (data protection) and has an in-depth knowledge and experience of this area of the law.

About the editor

Anne-Marie Mooney Cotter is a Montrealer, fluent in both English and French. She earned her Bachelors degree from McGill University at the age of 18, her Juris Doctor law degree from one of the leading Civil Rights Institutions, Howard University School of Law, and her Doctorate degree (PhD) from Concordia University in political economy international law on the issue of equality. Her work experience has been extensive, acting as Chief Advisor and later Administrative Law Judge appointed by the Prime Minister to the Veterans Review and Appeals Tribunal in Canada; Supervising Attorney in Alaska for the Legal Services Corporation in the United States, and later Executive Director; National Director for an Environmental Network in Canada; and is now Course Co-ordinator for Business Law at the Law Society of Ireland. Anne-Marie is a gold medallist in figure skating.

CONTENTS

About the Authors		v
Table of Cases		xiii
Table of Legislation		xv

1 INTRODUCTION TO INTELLECTUAL PROPERTY — 1
Carol Plunkett

1.1	Introduction	1
1.2	Intellectual property: what is it and what relevance does it have?	1
1.3	Areas of intellectual property	2
1.4	Current statutes	3
1.5	Historical background	3
1.6	Conclusion	6

2 TRADE MARKS — 7
Louise Carey and Maureen Daly

2.1	Introduction	7
2.2	What is a trade mark?	7
2.3	What type of mark can be registered?	7
2.4	Where should a trade mark be registered?	7
2.5	Who should do the filing of the application?	9
2.6	Registerability	9
2.7	Procedure before the Patents Office	11
2.8	The duration of the registration	11
2.9	Limitation on rights	11
2.10	Effects of registration	11
2.11	What constitutes 'infringing use'	12
2.12	What is not an infringement	12
2.13	Infringement proceedings	13
2.14	Section 24: groundless threats of infringement proceedings	13
2.15	Dealings with registered trade marks	14
2.16	Licensing	15
2.17	Exclusive licences	15
2.18	Non-exclusive licensees	15
2.19	Surrender, revocation and invalidity	16

2.20	Collective mark and certification mark	18
2.21	Famous marks	18
2.22	Offences	18
2.23	Jurisdiction	19
2.24	Community trade mark (CTM)	19

3 THE LAW OF PASSING OFF — 21
James Murray

3.1	Introduction	21
3.2	Core principles	21
3.3	Misrepresentation	22
3.4	Made by a trader in the course of trade	24
3.5	To prospective customers	24
3.6	Business or goodwill	25
3.7	Damage	26
3.8	The evolution of passing off: character merchandising	28
3.9	Personality rights	28
3.10	Practical steps in dealing with passing off	29

4 PATENTS — 31
Ken Parkinson and Andrew Parkes

4.1	Patent law	31
4.2	International conventions	31
4.3	Patentability	32
4.4	Ideas and know-how	36
4.5	Applying for a patent	36
4.6	Ownership of the right to a patent (ss 15–16, 79–80 of PA92)	38
4.7	Infringement (ss 40–46 of PA92)	40
4.8	Action for infringement	41
4.9	Remedies for infringement	42
4.10	Defences and statutory exceptions to infringement	44
4.11	Revocation	48
4.12	Amendment	49
4.13	Remedy for groundless threats	50
4.14	Declaration of non-infringement	50
4.15	The role of a patent agent in patent litigation	51
4.16	Miscellaneous matters	51

5 COPYRIGHT 1: THE COPYRIGHT AND RELATED RIGHTS ACT 2000 — 53
Rosaleen Byrne

5.1	Introduction and overview	53
5.2	Basic concepts of copyright law	57

6	**COPYRIGHT 2: THE ENFORCEMENT OF COPYRIGHT**	**67**
	Garrett Breen	
	6.1 Introduction	67
	6.2 Enforcement provisions in the 1963 Copyright Act (the 1963 Act)	67
	6.3 Infringement	67
	6.4 Substantial part	68
	6.5 Innocent infringement	69
	6.6 Primary and secondary infringement	69
	6.7 Remedies	70
	6.8 Offences	73
	6.9 Search warrants and seizure	74
7	**PROTECTION OF DATABASES AND COMPUTER PROGRAMS**	**75**
	Rosaleen Byrne	
	7.1 Protection of computer programs	75
	7.2 Protection of databases	81
	7.3 Summary	84
8	**INDUSTRIAL DESIGNS**	**85**
	Garrett Breen	
	8.1 Introduction	85
	8.2 Definition of design	86
	8.3 Protection of industrial designs	86
	8.4 Community design right	87
	8.5 What kind of design is registerable under the new 2001 Act?	88
	8.6 What does 'new' mean?	88
	8.7 Individual character	88
	8.8 Component parts	88
	8.9 Designs dictated by technical functions and designs of interconnections	88
	8.10 Ownership of a design	89
	8.11 Filing date	89
	8.12 Priority right	89
	8.13 When does registration take effect?	89
	8.14 What is a design right and what does it entitle the owner to do?	89
	8.15 Compulsory licences	90
	8.16 Infringement	90
	8.17 Remedies	90
	8.18 Groundless threats	90
	8.19 Rights of seizure and delivery up	90
	8.20 Offences	91
	8.21 Falsification of register	91
	8.22 Conclusion	91

9 INTELLECTUAL PROPERTY LICENCES — 93
Tara MacMahon

    9.1   Introduction — 93

    9.2   Recordal of licences — 94

    9.3   Competition law issues — 94

    9.4   Pre-contract considerations — 95

    9.5   Anatomy of a licence agreement — 95

    9.6   The tax treatment of licensing of intellectual property — 105

10 CONFIDENTIAL INFORMATION — 107
Carol Plunkett

    10.1 Introduction — 107

    10.2 Why should confidential information be protected? — 107

    10.3 History — 108

    10.4 Remedies — 112

11 CONCLUSION — 115
Maureen Daly

    11.1 Introduction — 115

    11.2 Future developments — 115

    11.3 Trade marks — 115

    11.4 Patents — 116

    11.5 Copyright — 116

    11.6 Stamp duty — 117

    11.7 Conclusion — 117

Index — 119

TABLE OF CASES

Ireland

A Modes Ltd v C & A Waterford Ltd [1978] SSR 126	3.6
adidas v Charles O'Neill and Co Ltd [1983] ILRM 112	3.3
An Post and Others v Irish Permanent [1995] IR 140	3.3
B & S Ltd v Irish Autotrader Ltd (Buy and Sell case) [1995] IR 142	3.3, 3.7
District Judge Martin [1993] ILR 651	6.2
Falcon Travel Ltd v Falcon Leisure Group [1991] IR 175	3.7
Gabicci plc v Dunnes Stores (High Court, 1991, unreported, Carroll J)	3.3
Guinness Ireland and Others v Kilkenny Brewing Co Ltd [1999] ILRM 531	3.6
Meadox Medicals v VPI Ltd and Denis Cummings and George Goicoechea (High Court, 1981, unreported, Hamilton J)	10.3.2
Merck & Co Inc v GD Searle & Co [2001] 2 ILRM 363	4.11
National Bank v RTÉ [1998] 2 IR 465	10.3.1
O'Neill's International Sports Co Ltd and Others v O'Neill's Footwear Dryer Co Ltd (High Court, 30 April 1997, unreported, Barron J)	3.6
Oblique Financial Services v Promise Production Co Ltd (1994) 1 PLRM 74	10.3.1
R Griggs Group Ltd and Others v Dunnes Stores (High Court, 1996, unreported, McCracken J)	3.3
Symonds Cider and Others v Showerings (Ireland) Ltd (Symonds case) [1997] 1 ILRM 482	3.5, 3.7

Europe

Deutsche Grammophon Gesellschaft mbH v Metro [1971] ECR 487	9.5.5
Marca Mode CV v Adidas AG and Adidas [2000] ETMR 723	2.10
Meck & Co Inc v Stepahr BV [1981] ECR 2063	9.5.5
Pharmon BV v Hoescht AG [1985] ECR 2281	9.5.5
Silhouette International Schmied GmbH and Co KG v Hartlauer [1998] ETMR 539	2.12
Van Zuylen Frères v Hag AG [1974] ECR 731	9.5.5

England and the Commonwealth

British Horseracing Board Ltd v William Hill Organisation Ltd [2001] 2 CMLR 12	7.2.5
Children's Television Workshop Inc v Woolworths (New South Wales) Ltd (Muppets case) [1981] RPC 187	3.8
Coco v Clarke [1969] RPC 41	10.3.1
Computer Associates v Altai [1992] 23 IPR 385	5.2.3
Dyson Appliances Ltd v Hoover Ltd [2001] RPC 544	4.9
Ervin Warnink BV v J Townsend and Sons (Hull) Ltd (Advocaat case) [1979] AC 731	3.2
Football League Ltd v Littlewood Pools Ltd [1950] Ch 637	7.2.1
Frances Day Hunter v Bron [1963] 2 All ER 16	6.4
Irvine v Talksport Ltd [2002] 1 All ER 214	3.9
John Richardson Computers Ltd v Flanders [1993] FSR 497	7.1.7
Kimberly-Clark v Procter & Gamble [2000] RPC 422	4.12
Krisarts SA v Briarfine Ltd [1977] FSR 557	6.4
Ladbroke v William Hill [1964] 1 WLR 237	5.2.3, 6.4
Mansell v Valley Printing Co [1908] 2 Ch 441	5.2.3
Newspaper Licensing Agency Ltd v Marks & Spencer [2000] 4 All ER 239	6.4
Norowzian v Arks Ltd [1999] FSR 79	5.2.2.1.2
Norwich Pharmacal Co v Customs & Excise Commissioners [1974] AC 133	4.16.2
Pasterfield v Denham and Another [1999] FSR 169	7.1.7
Pitney Bowes Inc v Francotyp-Postalia GmbH [1991] FSR 72, Ch D	4.10.2
Pope v Curl (1741) 26 ER 608	10.3
Prince Albert v Strange (1849) 1 Mac & G 25	1.5.5, 10.3
Ricordi v Clayton and Waller Ltd [1928] 35 MacCC 154	6.4
Ransburg-Gema AJ v Electrostatic Plant Systems Ltd [1991] FSR 508, CA	4.10.2
Saltman Engineering v Campbell Engineering [1948] 65 RPC 203; [1963] 2 All ER 413	10.3.1
Seager v Copydex (No 1) [1967] 2 All ER 415	10.3.1
Seager v Copydex (No 2) [1969] 2 All ER 718	10.3.1
Smith Kline & French Laboratories Ltd v Global Pharmaceuticals [1986] RPC 394	4.16.2
Terrapin v Builders Supply (Hayes) and Others [1960] RPC 128	10.3.1
University of London Press Ltd v University Tutorial Press Ltd [1916] 2 Ch 601	5.2.2.1, 5.2.2.1.1
Webb v Rose (1732) 98 ER 924	10.3
Wheatley (Davina) v Drillsafe Ltd [2001] RPC 133	4.7

TABLE OF LEGISLATION

Ireland

Statutes

Competition Act 2002—
  s 4 — 9.3
Continental Shelf Act 1968—
  s 1 — 4.7
Copyright Act 1963 — 1.5.1, 5.1, 5.1.1, 6.2
  s 27(4) — 6.2
Copyright Act 1977 — 6.2
Copyright (Amendment) Act 1987 — 5.1.1
Copyright and Related
  Rights Act 2000 — 1.4, 1.5.1, 5.1, 5.1.3, 5.2.2.1, 5.2.2.1.1, 6.1, 6.2, 6.7.2.1, 7.1.4, 7.1.7, 8.16, 8.17, 8.19
  s 2 — 5.2.2.1.2–5.2.2.1.4, 7.2, 7.2.2
  s 2(1) — 7.1.5, 7.1.6
  s 6 — 5.1.2
  s 17 — 5.2.1, 5.2.2
  s 17(1) — 5.2.1
  s 17(3) — 5.2.2, 7.1.6, 7.2.1
  s 17(4) — 5.2.2
  s 18(1) — 5.2.2.1.1
  s 18(2) — 5.2.2
  ss 21–23 — 7.1.7
  s 21 — 5.2.2.2
  s 22 — 5.2.2.2
  s 23(1) — 5.2.2.3
  s 23(2) — 5.2.2.3
  ss 24–36 — 5.1.2
  ss 24–30 — 5.2.2.4
  s 31(a) — 8.3
  ss 37–43 — 5.2.1
  s 37 — 5.2.3
  s 37(1) — 5.2.3, 7.1.8
  s 37(2) — 5.2.3, 6.3, 7.1.8
  s 37(3) — 5.2.3
  s 38 — 5.2.3
  s 39 — 5.1.5, 5.2.3, 5.2.3.1, 7.1.8, 7.1.9.3
  s 39(1) — 5.2.3.1
  s 39(1)(a) — 7.1.8.1

Copyright and Related Rights
  Act 2000 (contd)—
  s 39(2) — 5.2.3.1
  s 40 — 5.1.4, 5.1.5, 5.2.3, 5.2.3.2, 5.2.3.4, 7.1.8
  s 40(3) — 5.1.5
  s 41 — 5.2.3, 5.2.3.3, 7.1.8, 7.1.8.2
  s 41(2) — 5.2.3.3
  s 42 — 5.1.2, 5.2.3, 5.2.3.4, 7.1.8
  s 43 — 7.1.8
  s 43(2) — 7.1.8.3
  ss 44–48 — 5.2.1, 5.2.3.5
  s 44 — 6.6
  ss 45–48 — 6.6
  s 45 — 6.6.1
  s 47(1) — 6.6.1
  ss 80–82 — 5.1.5, 7.1.4
  s 80 — 7.1.8.1, 7.1.9.1
  s 81(1) — 7.1.9.2
  s 81(2) — 7.1.9.2
  s 82 — 7.1.8.1, 7.1.9.3
  s 82(2) — 7.1.9.3
  s 87 — 5.1.5, 7.1.8.1, 7.1.9.3
  ss 107–19 — 5.1.4
  ss 120–22 — 9.1.1
  s 122(1) — 9.1.1
  s 127 — 6.7.1
  s 128(2) — 6.5
  s 131 — 6.7.2.2, 6.7.2.3
  s 132 — 6.7.2.2, 6.7.2.3
  s 133 — 6.7.2.4
  s 135 — 9.1.1
  s 135(1) — 9.5.14
  s 136 — 9.1.1
  s 139 — 6.7.1
  s 139(2) — 6.7.1
  s 143 — 6.9
  s 145 — 6.7.2.2
  s 174 — 5.1.2
  ss 182–90 — 5.2.2
  ss 320–61 — 5.1.2
  s 320(1) — 7.2.4
  s 321 — 7.2.3

Statute	Reference
Copyright and Related Rights Act 2000 (contd)—	
s 324	7.2.4
s 324(3)	7.2.4
s 338	9.1.1, 9.5.14
ss 370–76	5.1.4
ss 370–74	5.1.5
ss 375–76	5.1.5
Pt I	5.2.2.4
Pt II	5.1.2
Pt III	5.2.2.1.2
Pt V	7.2, 7.2.2
Copyright Preservation Act 1929	1.5.1
Industrial and Commercial Property (Protection) Act 1927	1.5.1, 1.5.2, 1.5.4, 1.5.5, 4.1, 8.1–8.3, 8.14
Industrial Designs Act 2001	1.4, 1.5.2, 8.1, 8.2, 8.3
s 11	8.5
s 12	8.6
s 14	8.8
s 16	8.9
s 16(1)	8.9
s 16(2)	8.2, 8.9
s 19	8.10
s 26	8.12
s 42	8.14
s 50	8.16
s 56	8.18
s 63	8.9
s 87	8.3
Intellectual Property (Miscellaneous Provisions) Act 1998	5.1.1, 5.1.4
Maritime Jurisdiction Act 1959—	
s 5	4.7
Patents Act 1927	1.5.3
Patents Act 1964	1.5.3, 4.1
Patents Act 1992	1.4, 1.5.3, 4.1, 4.3.2, 9.5.9
s 9	4.3.1
s 9(1)	4.3.1
s 9(2)	4.3.1, 4.4
s 9(4)	4.3.1
s 9(5)	4.3.1
s 10	4.3.1
s 10(a)	4.3.1
s 11	4.3.1
s 11(1)	4.3.2
s 11(2)	4.3.2
s 11(3)	4.3.2
s 11(4)	4.3.2
Patents Act 1992 (contd)—	
s 12	4.3.2
s 13	4.3.2
s 14	4.3.1
s 15	4.6
s 16	4.6
s 16(2)	4.6
ss 18–22	4.5.2
s 18(1)	4.5.3
s 18(3)	4.5.3
s 18(2)	4.5.2
s 19	4.5.2
s 20	4.5.2, 4.12
s 21	4.5.2
ss 25–27	4.5.5
s 25	4.5.5
s 29	4.5.1, 4.5.3
s 30	4.5.3
s 32	4.12
s 32(2)	4.12
s 36(3)	4.9.1.1
s 37	4.10.6
s 37(7)	4.10.6
s 38	4.12
s 38(1)	4.12
s 38(2)	4.12
s 38(3)	4.12
s 38(5)	4.12
ss 40–46	4.7
s 40	4.7, 4.7.1, 4.7.2, 4.10.1
s 40(b)	4.7.2
s 41(1)	4.7.2
s 41(2)	4.7.2
s 42(a)	4.7.2, 4.10.7
s 42(b)	4.7.2, 4.10.8
s 42(c)	4.7.2, 4.10.9
s 43	4.10.2
s 44(3)	4.7.2
s 45(1)	4.7
s 45(3)	4.7
s 46	4.7
s 47	4.9
s 47(1)(a)	4.9.2
s 47(2)	4.9
s 49(1)	4.9.1.1
s 49(2)	4.9.1.1
s 50	4.9.3
s 50(2)	4.9.3
s 51	4.8, 4.9.1.1, 9.5.14
s 51(1)	4.8
s 51(2)	4.8
s 52	4.9.4
s 52(2)	4.9.4
s 53	4.13
s 54	4.14

TABLE OF LEGISLATION

Patents Act 1992 (contd)—	
s 55(1)	4.10.5
s 55(2)	4.10.5
s 57	4.11
s 57(5)	4.11
s 58	4.10.4, 4.11
s 58(c)	4.12
s 58(d)	4.12
s 59	4.11
ss 63–67	4.3.3
s 63(5)	4.5.3
s 66	4.3.3
s 66(1)	4.3.3
s 66(3)	4.3.3
ss 68–75	9.1.1
s 68(1)	4.10.10.3
s 68(2)(b)	4.10.10.3
ss 79–80	4.6
s 79	4.6.1
s 80	4.6.1
s 80(1)	4.6.1
s 80(2)	4.6.1
s 80(3)	4.6.1
s 80(4)	4.6.1
s 80(5)	4.6.1
s 80(6)	4.6.1
s 83	9.1.1
s 83(1)(a)	9.1.1
s 83(3)	9.5.9
s 83(4)	4.10.10.3
s 85(1)	9.2
s 85(3)	4.8
s 85(7)	4.8, 9.2, 9.5.14
s 94	4.16.1
s 95	4.8
s 95(2)	4.8
s 106(7)	4.16.1
s 117	4.7
ss 118–24	4.5.6
s 119	4.5.6
s 119(4)	4.5.6, 4.11
s 119(6)	4.5.6
s 127	4.5.7

Taxes Consolidation Act 1997—	
s 237	9.6.1
s 238	9.6.1
s 757(2)	9.6.4

Trade Marks Act 1963	1.5.4, 2.1
Trade Marks Act 1996	1.4, 1.5.4, 2.1, 2.4.3
s 6	2.2, 2.6.1
s 8	2.6.1, 2.19.3
s 8(1)(b)	2.19.3

Trade Marks Act 1996 (contd)—	
s 8(1)(c)	2.19.3
s 8(1)(d)	2.19.3
s 10	2.6.2
s 10(4)	2.6.2
s 13	2.10
s 14	2.10, 2.24.2
s 14(2)	2.10
s 14(3)	2.10
s 14(4)	2.11
s 14(5)	2.11
s 14(5)	2.11
s 14(6)	2.11
s 15(1)	2.12
s 15(2)(a)	2.12
s 15(2)(b)	2.12
s 15(2)(c)	2.12
s 15(3)	2.12
s 15(4)	2.12
s 16	9.5.5
ss 18–23	2.13
s 20	2.17, 2.23
s 22	2.13
s 23	2.15, 2.23
s 24	2.14
s 25	2.13
s 26	2.15
s 27	2.15
s 28	2.15
s 29(1)	2.15
s 29(2)	2.15
s 29(3)(a)	2.15, 9.2
s 29(3)(b)	2.15, 9.2
s 29(4)	2.15, 9.2
s 29(5)	2.15
ss 32–36	2.16, 9.1.1
s 32	9.1.1
s 32(1)	2.16, 2.17, 9.5.3
s 32(2)	2.16, 9.5.3
s 32(3)	2.16, 9.1.1
s 32(5)	2.16, 9.5.5
s 33	2.17
s 34	2.15, 2.18, 9.2, 9.5.14
s 34(2)	9.5.14
s 34(3)	9.5.14
s 35	2.15, 2.17, 9.2, 9.5.14
s 36	2.17, 9.5.14
s 36(2)	2.17
s 36(3)	2.17
s 36(4)	2.17
s 36(6)	2.17
s 40	2.7
s 47	2.8
s 48	2.8

Trade Marks Act 1996 (contd)—	
s 50	2.19.1
s 51	2.19.2
s 51(1)(a)	2.19.2
s 51(1)(b)	2.19.2
s 51(1)(c)	2.19.2
s 51(1)(d)	2.19.2
s 51(3)	2.19.2
s 52	2.19.3
s 52(4)	2.19.3
s 52(5)	2.19.3
s 52(6)	2.12, 2.19.3
s 53	2.19.3
s 54(1)	2.20
s 55(1)	2.20
s 61	2.21
s 61(2)	2.21
s 76	2.19.3
s 92(1)	2.22
s 92(3)	2.22
s 93	2.22
s 94	2.22
s 96	2.23
s 99	2.19.2
Sched 1	2.20
Sched 2	2.20
Value Added Tax Act 1972—	
Sched 4	9.6.2

Statutory Instruments

Community Design Regulations 2002 (SI 2002/2942)	8.4
European Communities (Counterfeit and Pirated Goods) Regulations 1996 (SI 1996/48)	2.13, 4.16.3
European Communities (Legal Protection of Biotechnological Inventions) Regulations 2000 (SI 2000/247)	4.1
European Communities (Legal Protection of Computer Programs) Regulations 1993 (SI 1993/26)	5.1.1, 5.1.2, 7.1.4
European Communities (Supplementary Protection Certificates) Regulations 1993 (SI 1993/125)	4.1, 4.3.4
European Communities (Term of Protection of Copyright) Regulations 1995 (SI 1995/158)	5.1.1
Patents Rules 1992 (SI 1992/172)	4.1
Rule 38	4.10.6
Rule 83	4.5.6
Rule 93(2)	4.5.3
Patents, Trade Marks and Designs (Fees) Rules 2001 (SI 2001/482)	4.1
Trade Marks (Madrid Protocol) Regulations 2001 (SI 2001/346)	2.4.3

Europe

Agreements, Treaties and Conventions

Agreement relating to Community Patents incorporating the Community Patent Convention 1975–89	4.2.4, 11.4
Berne Convention for the Protection of Literary and Artistic Works	
1971	1.5.1, 5.1.4, 5.2.2
Art 2	7.1.2
European Patent Convention	
1973	4.2.3, 4.3.1, 4.3.3, 4.5.3, 4.5.6, 4.12
Art 105a	4.12
Art 138(3)	4.12
Paris International Convention for the Protection of Industrial Property	
1883–1967	2.7, 4.2.1
Art 4	4.5.5
Patent Co-operation Treaty 1970	4.2.2, 4.3.3, 4.5.3, 4.5.7
Treaty of Rome Establishing the European Communities 1957 (as amended)	
Arts 28–30 (formerly Arts 30, 34 and 36)	4.10.2
Art 28 (formerly Art 30)	4.10.2
Art 30 (formerly Art 36)	4.10.2
Art 36 (formerly Art 42)	4.10.2
Art 81 (formerly Art 85)	5.1.2, 9.3
Art 81(1) (formerly Art 85(1))	4.10.2, 9.3
Art 82 (formerly Art 86)	4.10.2, 4.10.2, 5.1.2
World Copyright Treaty 1996	5.1.4, 5.1.5
Art 4	7.1.2
Art 8	5.2.3.2
World Phonograms and Performers Treaty 1996	5.1.4, 5.1.5
World Trade Organisation Agreement on Trade Related Aspects of Intellectual Property Rights (TRIPS)	5.1.1
Art 10(1)	7.1.2

Directives

77/388/EEC (Sixth Council Directive)	9.6.2
89/104/EEC (Trade Marks Harmonisation Directive)	2.1, 9.5.5
Art 7	9.5.5
91/250/EEC (Software Directive)	5.1.1, 5.1.2, 7.1.3, 7.1.4, 7.1.5
Art 1(2)	7.1.6
Art 1(3)	7.1.6
Art 6	7.1.9.2
92/100/EEC (Rental and Lending Directive)	5.1.2, 5.2.3.4
93/83/EEC (co-ordination of certain rules concerning copyright and rights relating to copyright applicable to satellite broadcasting and cable re-transmission)	5.1.2
93/98/EEC (Term Directive)	5.1.1, 5.1.2
96/9/EC (Database Directive)	5.1.2, 7.2, 7.2.4
01/29/EC (harmonisation of certain aspects of copyright and related rights in the Information Society)	5.1.3

Regulations

EEC/1768/92 (creation of a Supplementary Protection Certificate for medicinal products)	4.3.4
EU/40/94 (Community trade marks)	2.4.2, 11.3
Art 9	2.24.2
Art 93	2.24.3
EC/3295/94 (laying down measures to prohibit the release for free circulation, export, re-export or entry for a suspensive procedure of counterfeit and pirated goods)	4.16.3, 11.3
EC/240/96 (Technology Transfer Block Exemption)	4.4, 9.3, 9.5.8, 9.5.11, 9.5.17
EC/1610/96 (creation of a Supplementary Protection Certificate for plant protection products)	4.3.4
EC/241/99 (amending Regulation EC/3295/94 laying down measures to prohibit the release for free circulation, export, re-export or entry for a suspensive procedure of counterfeit and pirated goods)	4.16.3
EC/2790/99 (Vertical Agreements Block Exemption)	9.3

England

Statutes

Copyright Act 1911	1.5.1
Copyright Act 1956	1.5.1
Copyright of Design Act 1839	1.5.2
Design Act 1842	1.5.2
Designing and Printing of Linen Act 1787	1.5.2
Engraving Copyright Act 1734	1.5.1
Fine Arts Copyright Act 1862	1.5.1
Licensing Act 1662	1.5.1
Patent Law Amendment Act 1852	1.5.3
Patents Act 1902	1.5.3
Patents Act 1949	1.5.3
Statute of Monopolies 1624	1.5.3
Trade Marks Act 1905	1.5.4
Trade Marks Act 1948	1.5.4
Trade Marks Registration Act 1875	1.5.4

United States of America

Statutes

Computer Software Copyright Act 1980	7.1.1
Digital Millennium Copyright Act 2000	5.1.5

CHAPTER 1

INTRODUCTION TO INTELLECTUAL PROPERTY

Carol Plunkett

1.1 Introduction

This intellectual property text is designed to equip you as a solicitor with a practical knowledge of all areas of intellectual property law. The text has been written by practitioners who advise clients in these areas of law. The chapters are at a reasonably advanced level and are designed to give you sufficient knowledge to advise your clients in each of the different areas. Your clients will often confuse patents, copyright and trade marks. They will discuss how they want to register their copyright or patent their trade mark, and, indeed, lawyers often make the same mistake. This text will hopefully ensure that you are not one of them!

This introductory chapter will set the background against which all of the technical aspects to the following 10 chapters is set. This chapter is more for cultural interest than for education. It gives an explanation of what intellectual property is, the different categories and which type of properties fit into which category, together with an outline of the historical background showing how the law has evolved in this area.

1.2 Intellectual property: what is it and what relevance does it have?

There is no precise definition of intellectual property, because it is a basket of different rights and is as diverse as human ingenuity. Intellectual property is a product of the human intellect. It may be an invention, a concept, a literary or artistic creation, a computer program or process, a design, an industrial process or method, a unique name or brand, or a piece of information which is confidential. All of these things just mentioned can be called pieces of property. All can have features which are unique, novel, and which are not obvious. They are the fruit of the creative endeavour of human beings.

As time has evolved, this creative intellectual endeavour or innovation has been recognised, has been given the name 'intellectual property' (before that 'industrial property') and has been divided into the various categories discussed later. Legal rights have been granted to protect what is largely intangible property, but which has been given substance by law or what one might describe as 'virtual' substance to assist its owner in exploiting it and in defending it against pirates.

Although the term 'intellectual property' is a relatively recent term, it does not take much imagination to realise that because its very basis is innovation, it has existed since the first man stepped onto earth and discovered fire or invented the wheel. However, it has taken thousands of years for the law to begin to recognise this innovation and to go some way towards encouraging innovation by protecting it. In recent years, this intangible property has been recognised by businesses as being an extremely valuable asset. Some companies rely entirely upon intellectual property for their profit. Examples of these are:

(a) information technology companies, such as Microsoft and Apple, which rely on copyright to protect their innovation in the software industry;
(b) companies such as Coca Cola, or Pepsi Cola, who need to protect the formula for a soft drink, the recipes for which are confidential information;
(c) companies such as Waterford Wedgewood, adidas, Gucci or Ferrari, who rely upon their brand name to enhance the value of their product.

These intellectual property rights are assets of unquantifiable value and produce billions of dollars for their owners.

Having said that, it is not just companies known worldwide which have intellectual property as one of their assets. Any business with a name has an asset worth protecting and about which they should be seeking legal advice. More and more companies are ensuring that their intellectual property forms a part of their balance sheet and is an asset which can be mortgaged or charged to assist in raising capital and which should be protected. Lawyers form a necessary evil in that process, if not a vital cog.

It is therefore extremely important that any solicitor advising a client on any aspect of commercial law is in a position to advise on intellectual property aspects, whether to give guidance in relation to the registration of the intellectual property, its assignment or licensing or defence of it, or being able to carry out a due diligence of the property in the event that it is being sold or charged. The property is an asset and can be dealt with in just the same manner as any real or personal property. It can be exploited as its owner decides, by sale, by licence or by mortgage. The property can be given away as a gift, disposed of in a will and can be treated exactly as if it were a piece of tangible property. Most of those dealings require the advice and assistance of a solicitor.

This then is the relevance of intellectual property. In short, intellectual property can be defined as the intangible or tangible results of the creative endeavour and innovation of human beings.

1.3 Areas of intellectual property

Intellectual property is at present divided into four main statutory categories and two common law categories. The statutes confer upon the owner of each intellectual property right a monopoly in the property protected.

The categories into which intellectual property is divided include the following:

(a) Copyright and industrial design, which protect the physical form of literary, dramatic, musical and artistic endeavour. Computer software is included in this category. This is the area covering books, music and the performing arts, as well as sculpture, architectural drawings, buildings, designs, patterns and so on.
(b) Patents, which protect inventions, like the Zip fastener, the Bic biro, the Tetrapak and pharmaceuticals.
(c) Trade marks, which protect names used in the course of trade and in the provision of services. A trade mark can be a name, a logo, a picture, a shape, or even a smell (if it can be described in words).
(d) Passing off, which protects in common law the goodwill and reputation of a business.
(e) Confidential information, where again under common law an obligation of confidentiality exists in relation to information imparted from one party to another.

It cannot be emphasised enough how important it is, when advising a client, to read each specific statute first. Often, cases in this area of the law are decided on the precise wording of a particular section of the relevant act and the sections are not necessarily set out in a chronological or logical order.

1.4 Current statutes

The current statutes are the Patents Act 1992, the Trade Marks Act 1996, the Copyright and Related Rights Act 2000 and the Industrial Designs Act 2001. Each of these will be discussed in detail in this text. First, however, the background of intellectual property and how this concept has evolved is discussed.

1.5 Historical background

1.5.1 Copyright

The first category to be considered in a historical context is that of copyright, since it appears to be the oldest area which was protected. The right to be recognised as the author of a particular work was claimed long ago by scholars in ancient Greece and the Roman Empire.

Irish text books on the topic of copyright tell of the tale of St Columcille, who is alleged to have copied a gospel manuscript which belonged to St Fintan, without his consent. St Fintan reported the matter to Dairmait, High King of Ireland who sat, listened to the evidence and gave judgment in the matter. The King found for St Fintan and ruled that 'for every cow its calf' and 'to every book its copy'. Some writers say that this is a complete fairytale, but nonetheless it is a good place to start looking at the history of copyright. The repeal of the Brehon Laws in Ireland by King James I resulted in a certain lawlessness in this jurisdiction and copyright is no exception to this.

With the invention of printing at the end of the 15th century, a form of copyright protection began to develop in the United Kingdom. Since books could be printed rather than copied in manuscript, illicit publishing mushroomed and began to adversely affect the economic rights of the legitimate publishing industry. In England, the King attempted to control what was printed, by establishing a Register at Stationers Hall, in which every book published was listed. After several royal charters, the Licensing Act of 1662 gave the Stationers Company powers to seize books, establish printing presses and publish books. The Star Chamber incorporated a company known as 'the Masters and Keepers, or Wardens and Commonality of the Mystery and Art of the City of London' and gave to that company the power to search for and seize illicit printing presses, letters or other materials for printing.

By 1681, the Licensing Act had been repealed and although the right to make copies of books was vested in the stationer, the manuscript was held under a common law copyright by the author. However, this was an unsatisfactory situation and the Stationers Company had no control over the publication of books in Scotland or in Ireland. Further, no common law copyright existed in Scotland and the industry campaigned for property rights in literary works.

This eventually resulted in the passing of the Statute of Anne, which was the first copyright act giving the author the right to claim ownership of copyright in a work and granting a fixed term of protection for published works. It became law on 10 April 1710. The period of protection was 14 years from first publication and this could be extended if the owner was alive for a further 14 years. The matter was complicated by the fact that the first period of 14 years protected the owner, who in all likelihood was a publisher, whereas the second period of 14 years was a right granted to the author. This led to a good deal of litigation as to who was entitled to what.

Not the least of the questions that were litigated was when was a book a book. Music sheets were held to be books and dramatic works also came within the concept of a book. William Hogarth succeeded in persuading Parliament to pass the Engraving Copyright Act in 1734. This Act also extended the period of protection and in 1814 statutory copyright in published books was extended to a period of 28 years or the author's life, whichever was longer.

Copyright in sculptures, maps, charts and plans followed in subsequent legislation and no registration of these was required at Stationers Hall. The Fine Arts Copyright Act in 1862 covered paintings, drawings and photographs for the life of the author and seven years after death.

Then, on 1 July 1912, the Copyright Act 1911 brought provisions on copyright under one umbrella for the very first time. That act dispensed with the requirement to register copyright. It also incorporated provisions, which complied with the Berne Convention on copyright worldwide, and modern copyright was born.

In Ireland, with the coming of the Irish Free State, copyright was cast into limbo when the Supreme Court held that the Copyright Act 1911 did not form part of Irish law. In a case brought by the Performing Rights Society (which protected composers and music publishers and was established in 1914) against Bray Urban District Council, the Supreme Court held that the unauthorised performance by a band of a musical work on Bray seafront was not an infringement. This led to the Copyright Preservation Act 1929, but subsequently the Privy Council held that the Supreme Court was wrong and that the 1911 Act did remain in force until repealed by the Oireachtas by the Industrial and Commercial Property (Protection) Act 1927.

Unfortunately from then until last year, copyright protection in Ireland lagged behind other jurisdictions. The Copyright Act 1963 was borrowed largely from the UK Copyright Act 1956 and although it served us very well, it has been described as an excellent example of 'how not to proceed' to draft an Act. Ireland is now the proud owner of the Copyright and Related Rights Act 2000.

1.5.2 Designs

With the start of the industrial revolution, copyright was extended to industrial designs and the Designing and Printing of Linen Act 1787 protected, for a period of two months, the owner of work in the 'arts of designing and printing linens, cottons, calicos and muslin'. In 1839, a system of registration was introduced by the Copyright of Design Act and fabric comprised of wool, silk or hair came within its ambit together with protection far beyond the textile trade to every new or original design ornamentation and the share or configuration of any article of manufacture.

The Design Act 1842 consolidated earlier legislation and included functional features so that springs for a bicycle, an oil can and gas pilot light were capable of registration. Then in Ireland, the Industrial and Commercial Property (Protection) Act 1927 was enacted. It governed designs until it was replaced by the Industrial Designs Act 2001.

1.5.3 Patents

The British claim to have the longest continuous patent tradition in the world. However, in Venice towards the end of the 15th century, protection was granted to inventions for a 10-year term. In Britain, the Crown granted privileges to manufacturers and traders marked by letters patent, which were literally letters with the King's Great Seal affixed to them.

In 1449, Henry VI granted John of Utynam the earliest known English patent for a method of making stained glass for the windows of Eton College. During Tudor times, monopolies were granted for trades and manufacturers including letters patent for inventions. Apparently, Elizabeth I granted about 50 patents for monopolies in the sale of soap, saltpetre, alum, leather, salt, glass, knives, sail cloth, sulphur, starch and paper. The UK Patent Office website refers to Sir John Harrington's request for a patent on his design for a water closet being turned down in 1596 on the grounds of impropriety.

During the reign of James I, English law became legally established in Ireland. King James revoked all previous patents in 1610 and declared that 'monopolies are things contrary to our laws' (probably the earliest statement of competition law) except for 'projects of new invention so they be not contrary to the law, nor mischievous to the state'. His words were incorporated into the Statute of Monopolies 1624, the first recognisable patents act.

During the reign of Queen Anne, a requirement was introduced that the patentee must, by an instrument in writing, describe and ascertain the nature of the invention and the manner in which it is to be performed. Mr James Puckle's patent in 1718 for a machine gun was one of the first patents to provide a 'specification' the word used for the specification of an invention. The system was complicated however and a person wishing to obtain a patent had to present a petition to seven offices and pay substantial fees.

Charles Dickens wrote a spoof article called 'A Poor Man's Tale of a Patent' which was published in a journal called 'Household Words'. Dickens' inventor apparently visited 34 offices, including some abolished years before, in his pursuit of the grant of a patent.

The Great Exhibition of 1851 produced the impetus for the amendment of patent law. The Patent Law Amendment Act 1852 established a single patent office for England, Scotland and Ireland, simplified the procedure, reduced the legal fees and made provision for single UK patent granting protection for England, Scotland, Wales, Ireland, Channel Islands and the Isle of Man. A subsequent amendment in 1883 established the Controller General of Patents and a system of examiners to ensure that the specification described the invention properly.

Then, in 1902, the Patents Act introduced examination as to the novelty of an invention. Examiners were required to search through UK specifications over the previous 50 years. This of course, without the aid of computers, required a huge amount of work. Two hundred and sixty examiners were employed to search through 1022 volumes of abridged patent specifications, arranged in 146 classes according to subject. By 1907, the abridgement volumes went back as far as Patent No 1 of 1617, granted to Rathburn & Burges for 'engraving and printing maps, plans etc'.

With the coming of the Irish Free State in 1921 and the entering into limbo of intellectual property, there was no Patents Act in Ireland until the 1927 Act. One of the requirements for obtaining a valid patent is that the invention is new. If it has been published before, then this element of novelty is lost. One of the interesting provisions in the 1927 Act was that publication was limited to within the State, so that it was possible for inventions which had been patented in other jurisdictions to be patented in the Irish Free State by 'the first party to introduce or import the invention into the Irish Free State'. In 1964, a new Patents Act was published in Ireland, which was very similar to the UK Patents Act 1949. The current Patents Act is that of 1992.

1.5.4 Registered trade marks and passing off

Marking goods in a way to distinguish them from those of other manufacturers can be traced back to ancient times. In the medieval era, crafts and trades guilds introduced rules for the marking of goods. The common law remedy of passing off was also evolving.

Originally, marks were used to denote ownership or for regulatory purposes, to set standards of quality as delimited by the traders who formed guilds or unions of their industries in London. In the 18th century, various cases are reported in which the plaintiff seeks in injunction to restrain a defendant from using a mark the same as the plaintiff's, but always on the basis that the defendant was in some way fraudulent in his use, so that the use adversely affected the plaintiff's reputation.

However, it was only early in the 19th century that the concept of a mark being distinctive and identifying a particular trader's goods, attracting goodwill and being considered as a piece of property arose. The courts at that time also allowed the owner of such a mark to take an action for infringement of his mark, even where there was no intention to deceive on the part of the infringer. The law made substantial developments in the 19th century and, during the 1860s, the courts began to recognise that trade marks were a form of property.

In particular, Lord Westbury found that as soon as a mark was used in trade, a right of property came into existence and that this could be enforced on an equitable basis, even against an innocent infringer. The Trade Marks Registration Act 1875 made provision for a legal register of trade marks and the first trade marks registry in the world opened in London in 1876. The Act of 1875 did not provide for an action for infringement. The assumption was made that this right already existed both in equity and at common law. The courts after 1875 enforced the new registered trade marks even in the absence of any statutory provision, but the Trade Marks Act 1905 introduced statutory provisions for infringement and also stated that nothing in it affected the action for passing off.

Registration of a trade mark gives the owner of the mark an exclusive right to use that mark, to sue for infringement and to stop third parties from using the mark without the owner's consent. Thus, the law of trade marks and of passing off were permitted to develop independently of each other, and the last quarter of the 19th century defined much of the law that still applies today.

In Ireland, the Industrial and Commercial Property (Protection) Act 1927 made provision for the setting up of the Irish Trade Marks Office. The first trade mark to be advertised in the Irish official journal was 'Déanta In Eirinn', a logo owned by the Industrial Development Association. Trade mark law in Ireland evolved with the introduction of the Trade Marks Act 1963, which was extremely similar to the UK Trade Marks Act 1948. Then in 1996, the current Trade Marks Act came into force which provides for marks in respect of services, as well as use in the course of trade. It is also now possible to apply for a community trade mark to the Trade Marks Office in Alicante so as to obtain a mark which is registered throughout the European Union.

1.5.5 Confidential information

The area of confidential information is still developing and the case law in relation to it is relatively modern. This is not a statutory area and the textbooks refer to the first case in which the duty of confidence was recognised as being *Prince Albert v Strange* in 1849 (1 Mac & G 25), which involved etchings belonging to the Royal Family. These came into the possession of a Mr Strange who arranged them in a catalogue for exhibition. An injunction was granted to restrain this. Since then the law has been substantially refined and is discussed in detail later.

1.6   Conclusion

This then is the scene set for the following chapters.

CHAPTER 2

TRADE MARKS

Louise Carey and Maureen Daly

2.1 Introduction

Trade mark law in Ireland is currently governed by the Trade Marks Act 1996 (the 1996 Act). The 1996 Act, which implements the Trade Marks Harmonisation Directive 89/104/EEC, became operative as and from 1 July 1996. Prior to this date, the Trade Marks Act 1963 was applicable. The 1963 Act is still applicable in certain circumstances but for the purpose of this article, reference will be made to the provisions of the 1996 Act as it is this legislation that is most commonly used nowadays.

2.2 What is a trade mark?

Put at its simplest, a trade mark is some type of sign which distinguishes the product or service of one manufacturer or service provider from another. Well-known trade marks, such as 'Flake', 'Oxo' or the 'Michelin Man character', are extremely valuable assets for the companies who own them. The key feature of a trade mark is that it is 'distinctive' of that product or service and no one else's product, so that it serves as a 'badge of origin' and as a type of guarantee to the consumer as to the origin of that product.

A great many people mistakenly believe that if a trade mark is not registered then it is not legally protected. This is not the case if the mark in question has been put to significant use in trade such that it has become well-known and has thus accrued a 'reputation' and 'goodwill'. Such an unregistered trade mark will then be protected in Ireland by the law of passing off.

2.3 What type of mark can be registered?

According to s 6 of the 1996 Act, practically any kind of distinctive sign can be registered, provided it is capable of being represented graphically. Most commonly, trade marks consist of words, 'devices' (sometimes referred to as 'logos') and shapes. However, s 6 lists as possible trade marks: words (including personal names), designs, letters, numerals or the shape of goods or their packaging.

2.4 Where should a trade mark be registered?

Currently, there are four possibilities for registration, namely:

(a) national filing at the Irish Patents Office, Hebron Road, Kilkenny;
(b) filing for a community trade mark (CTM) at the Office for Harmonisation in the Internal Market (OHIM) in Alicante, Spain;

(c) Madrid Protocol filing;

(d) selective filings in individual countries.

The relative merits of each of these options are dealt with in the following sections.

2.4.1 Irish national filing

This is the cheapest option, and is best suited to a proprietor whose mark is only used in Ireland. It is possible to apply in a single application to register one mark in several classes of goods or services by paying additional fees per additional class. Marks are classified according to the 'Nice Classification' (this can be accessed at the Patents Office website www.patentsoffice.ie). For example, a person might wish to protect a mark for use in regard to soft drinks, coffee and t-shirts, in which case the filing should be made in classes 32, 30 and 25. Provided an applicant has an Irish address they can file the application personally but a solicitor must be registered at the Patents Office as a trade mark agent in order to be able to process trade mark filings.

2.4.2 Office for Harmonisation in the Internal Market (OHIM)

The 1996 Act gave effect to Council Regulation EU/40/94 (the Regulation) on the community trade mark. Since April 1996, applications have been filed at the OHIM in Alicante, Spain to obtain 'community trade marks' (CTMs). The principal advantage to this type of protection is that a mark can be protected in all Member States of the European Union by a single registration. Disadvantages are that the costs of registration are greater, and as the registration system is an 'all or nothing' system, it means that it is not possible to hold a CTM registration excluding one or more European Union countries. Therefore, an earlier trade mark on one of the national registers in a European Union country or indeed on the Community Trade Mark Register itself can form the basis of an opposition before OHIM. If the opposition is successful, the applicant can either abandon the application, or alternatively convert it into a series of national applications which will still enjoy the same filing date as the original CTM application (see section 2.4.4 below).

2.4.3 The Madrid Protocol

The 1996 Act also gave effect to the 'Madrid Protocol'. The Protocol was implemented by the Trade Marks (Madrid Protocol) Regulations 2001 (SI 2001/346), which came into operation on 19 October 2001. The gist of this system is that once the trade mark owner is domiciled or is a national or has a real commercial base in a Protocol country (eg, Ireland) and his mark is the subject of an application or registration in the home country (eg, Ireland) (the 'basic application or registration'), the trade mark owner can choose or 'designate' in which of the Protocol countries the registration (known as an 'international registration') is to take effect. An application is filed at the Irish Patents Office and once examined as to formalities, it is forwarded to the International Bureau of the World Intellectual Property Organisation (WIPO) in Geneva. The WIPO office records the mark in its 'International Register', and then notifies the mark to the Trade Mark Offices of each designated country. However, these designated country offices can refuse protection to the mark, and the trade mark owner can contest this refusal at the local office. Even if a country is deleted from the application, the international application will (notwithstanding this) proceed in respect of the balance of the countries designated by the applicant. The risk with a Madrid Protocol filing is that if the 'basic' application or registration fails or is cancelled within the first five years of the initial 10-year term of the International Registration, then the latter also fails. However, if this occurs, the proprietor may convert the international registration into a series of national applications, which retain the date of filing of the international registration. Such a conversion must occur within three months of the loss of the international registration. After five years, the International Register is independent of the 'basic' application/registration.

2.4.4 Selective filings in individual countries

Frequently, traders use their trade mark only in Ireland and perhaps one or two other countries. In such a case, it may be cheaper and easier to file in each relevant country at the national Patents Office. The foreign country filings will then have to be done through local agents.

2.5 Who should do the filing of the application?

A solicitor who is also a registered trade mark agent at the Patents Office can file trade mark applications in Ireland. To file at the OHIM in Spain, one must also be a registered representative. Irish trade mark agents are accepted for registration as representatives by the OHIM. The filing and prosecution of trade mark applications can in some circumstances be very straightforward, if no official objections on the mark's registrability are encountered and there is no third party opposition to the registration. However, dealing with official objections and oppositions requires a detailed up-to-date knowledge of the applicable statutory and case law.

2.6 Registerability

An important issue to be aware of, for the purposes of the registrability of a mark, is that a mark can be refused registration by the Patents Office on the basis of what are known as 'absolute' and 'relative' grounds. Each of these grounds will be examined separately below in order to understand the basis on which an application can be refused registration.

2.6.1 Absolute grounds

Under s 8 of the 1996 Act, an application can be refused registration by an Examiner at the Patents Office if the following criteria are not met:

(a) the mark is not a trade mark as defined in s 6;
(b) the mark is devoid of any distinctive character;
(c) the mark consists exclusively of signs or indications which may serve in the trade to designate the kind, quality, quantity, intended purpose, value, geographical origin, time of production of goods or of rendering of services, or other characteristics of goods or services;
(d) the mark consists exclusively of signs or indications which have become customary in the current language or in the *bona fide* and established practices of the trade.

Notwithstanding the above criteria, an application for registration of a mark may still be accepted by the Patents Office even though it falls foul of (b)–(d) above. If the applicant can show to the satisfaction of the Patents Office that the mark has acquired a distinctive character as a result of substantial usage prior to the date of application, the trade mark application will be allowed to proceed.

In addition to the above, a mark cannot be registered if it consists exclusively of a shape which results from nature of the goods, a shape which is necessary to obtain a technical result or a shape which gives substantial value to the mark. Also, a mark cannot be registered if it is contrary to public policy or accepted principles of morality, or if it is of such a nature so as to deceive the public, for instance as to the nature, quality or geographic origin of the goods or services.

Also, a mark cannot be registered if its use is prohibited in the state by any enactment or rule of law or if the application itself was made in bad faith. A mark consisting of a State Emblem of Ireland cannot be registered, unless the requisite consent has been granted by the Minister. This protection for emblems also extends to those of a public authority, unless the requisite consent has been obtained.

From each of the above objections, it is clearly evident that a mark cannot be registered if it is one that should be open to use by the public or indeed by other traders in the industry for which the mark is to be used. This protection also extends to marks that might be deceptive. Concern is also had for marks that are contrary to public policy or accepted principles of morality and examples of this would occur in situations where the marks would be likely to cause offence to a section of the public on the grounds of race, religious belief or even general matters of taste and decency.

2.6.2 Relative grounds

Relative grounds are raised by an Examiner where there are earlier trade mark rights for which protection should be granted. There are three circumstances in which objections on relative grounds (which can be found in s 10 of the 1996 Act) will be raised and these circumstances are as follows:

(a) the trade mark is 'identical' to the earlier mark and the goods or services for which the mark is to be applied are also 'identical' to the goods or services for which the earlier mark is protected;

(b) the mark is 'identical/similar' to the earlier mark and the goods or services which protection is sought are also 'similar/identical or similar' to the goods or services for which the earlier mark is protected *and* there is a likelihood of confusion on the part of the public which includes the likelihood of association;

(c) a mark is 'identical/similar' to an earlier mark but the goods or services in respect of both marks are 'dissimilar' *but* the earlier mark has a reputation in the State (or in the case of a CTM, in the Community) and the use of the later trade mark without due cause would take unfair advantage of or be detrimental to the distinctive character or reputation of the earlier trade mark.

In addition to the above circumstances, a mark can be opposed by an earlier trade mark owner under s 10(4) of the 1996 Act, to the extent that he can prove that the use of the later mark would be prevented under the law of passing off. Obviously, during the course of a trade mark examination, this will not be raised by an Examiner, because he would be unaware of the existence of such rights. However, in practice this provision is cited by an opponent who relies upon unregistered rights in opposition proceedings before the Patents Office.

Having looked at the basis on which an Examiner can object to the registration of a trade mark, let us now look at the actual procedure for registering a mark in Ireland.

2.7 Procedure before the Patents Office

When an application for registration is filed at the Patents Office, it is assigned an official filing number. The information required for filing an application is:

(a) name and address of the applicant;

(b) details of the trade mark;

(c) the classes of goods or services, in respect of which the mark is to be registered;

(d) an address for service in the State, ie the address of a trade mark agent/solicitor.

Under s 40 of the 1996 Act, if the mark has already been filed in a country, which is a member of the 'Paris Convention' and priority is claimed from that application (that is, the Irish application is filed within six months of that application), the filing date of the Irish application is deemed to be the date of the filing of the application in the Convention country.

Once filed, the application joins a queue of applications that await formal examination by an Examiner. If the Examiner has any questions as to the mark's registerability, an official report will be issued and if the proprietor can address the questions to the satisfaction of the Examiner, the application will proceed to advertisement in the *Official Journal*, which is issued by the Patents Office to all Irish trade mark agents and which is published. At this stage, third parties will have the opportunity to oppose the application, such opposition to be filed within three months of the date of advertisement. This deadline date is 'non-extendible'. If there is no third party opposition, the mark will proceed to registration upon payment of the registration fee.

The procedure indicated above is identical to the procedure for registering CTMs before OHIM. However, when CTM applications are being examined, they are only examined on 'absolute grounds'.

2.8 The duration of the registration

Registered trade marks (be they national Irish marks or CTMs) are registered initially for a 10-year period, but, uniquely among intellectual property rights, this term can be renewed indefinitely for successive 10-year terms, on payment of a renewal fee (s 47 of the 1996 Act). If a national mark is not renewed, s 48 of the 1996 Act provides for the possible late renewal or even restoration, if the mark has already been taken off the Register.

2.9 Limitation on rights

A trade mark registration will only remain valid to the extent that the mark is used by the owner in respect of the goods or services for which it was registered. Failure to use a mark will render the registration vulnerable to cancellation on the grounds of non-use. This attack will only arise after the mark has been registered for five years. Thereafter, a cancellation action can be instituted.

2.10 Effects of registration

The registration of a trade mark in Ireland gives the trade mark proprietor the exclusive right to use that trade mark in Ireland in respect of the goods or services for which it is registered (s 13 of the 1996 Act).

Accordingly, if another person uses that mark without consent, that usage will infringe the rights of the proprietor. Such rights arise from the date of registration of the mark, which is deemed to be the date the application was filed.

Section 14 sets out the criteria for infringement of the registration. In summary, an infringement will occur where a mark, which is the same or similar to a registered mark, is used in relation to the same or similar goods or services as the registered mark. Section 14(2) refers to the infringing use creating a 'likelihood of confusion ... which includes a likelihood of association'. The interpretation of this has been scrutinised by the ECJ in a number of important cases, the most recent of which is C-425/98 *Marca Mode CV v Adidas AG and Adidas* [2000] ETMR 723. The upshot of these cases is that the concept of 'likelihood of association' is not an alternative to that of likelihood of confusion, but serves to define its scope.

Section 14(3) provides for infringement occurring where an identical or similar mark is used in relation to goods or services, which are not similar to those for which the registered trade mark is registered, provided the registered trade mark has a reputation in the State and the unwarranted use of the infringing mark takes unfair advantage of or is detrimental to the distinctive character or reputation of the registered trade mark. This is a new provision introduced by the 1996 Act.

2.11 What constitutes 'infringing use'

Section 14(4) sets out examples of unauthorised acts, which will infringe a registered mark. The list is not exhaustive. Affixing the mark to goods or their packaging, selling goods or supplying services under the mark, importing or exporting goods under the mark, or using the mark on business papers or in advertising are all actions which will be deemed to be infringements of the registered mark. Section 14(5) provides for a person who knowingly applies an infringing mark to labelling or packaging materials or to business papers or advertising materials to be deemed to be an infringer.

Section 14(6) radically changed the law by permitting 'comparative advertising'. This is where a trader compares his product to that of a competitor and in doing so explicitly refers to the competitor's product by its trade mark. This was not permitted in the past but is now allowed, provided it is in accordance with 'honest practices in industrial or commercial matters'.

2.12 What is not an infringement

The following are not infringements of trade marks:

(a) use of another registered mark which is valid (s 15(1) and s 52(6) of the 1996 Act);
(b) use of a person's name or address (s 15(2)(a) of the 1996 Act);
(c) use of purely descriptive indications (eg, quantity, geographical origin) (s 15(2)(b) of the 1996 Act);
(d) use of the registered mark to explain the purpose of another product, for example, an accessory made to fit a BMW car (s 15(2)(c) of the 1996 Act);
(e) use of a prior or earlier unregistered mark, which has been in continuous use since before either the first use or registration of the registered mark and the earlier mark has a goodwill which would be protected by the law of passing off (s 15(3), (4) of the 1996 Act). This is a very important provision, which frequently turns up in practice. 'Goodwill' basically means the power the mark has to attract customers due to its renown and reputation;
(f) in general, infringement will not occur where the trade mark rights have been 'exhausted'. This occurs where the registered mark is put onto goods in another

country in the European Economic Area (EEA) by the trade mark owner or with his consent, and which after the first sale, are resold and circulated from there into Ireland. The registered mark in Ireland cannot be invoked in that situation to stop the 'parallel importing' of the goods, unless the condition of the goods has been changed in some way since first marketing (s 16(l), (2) of the 1996 Act). It should be noted that it is possible to use national trade mark rights to stop such parallel imports from countries outside the EEA: Case C-355/96 *Silhouette International Schmied GmbH and Co KG v Hartlauer* [1998] ETMR 539, decision of 16 July 1998.

2.13 Infringement proceedings

These are covered exhaustively in ss 18–23 of the 1996 Act. The reliefs available are:

(a) damages;
(b) an injunction;
(c) an account of the defendant's profits;
(d) an order for erasure, removal or obliteration of the infringing sign;
(e) an order for destruction of the goods if erasure etc is not possible;
(f) an order for delivery up to the plaintiff of the infringing goods (this is subject to a six-year time limit: s 22);
(g) an order for disposal (ie, destruction or forfeiture to a particular person).

In most litigation concerning trade mark infringement, the pleadings will almost certainly claim damages, and as an alternative, an account of profits, and usually a permanent injunction.

Pursuant to s 25 of the 1996 Act, the District Court has the power to order the seizure without warrant of infringing goods, to grant a warrant for the search for and seizure of infringing goods, and also to order their subsequent delivery up or destruction.

The Customs Authorities pursuant to the European Communities (Counterfeit and Pirated Goods) Regulations 1996 (SI 1996/48) have the power to seize counterfeit goods at the behest of the trade mark proprietor, who has submitted evidence of ownership of the requisite intellectual property.

2.14 Section 24: groundless threats of infringement proceedings

Under s 24 of the 1996 Act, where a person threatens another with proceedings for infringement, the person aggrieved may apply to court for relief for groundless threats. This provision is not applicable where the infringement is set to arise out of the application of the mark to the goods, the importation of goods to which the mark has been applied or the supply of services under the mark. Relief available to the complainant is an injunction to stop the threats from continuing, a declaration that the threats are unjustified, and damages sustained as a result of the threats.

If such proceedings are instituted, the registered owner will find themselves losing the initiative and be forced into defending costly litigation and will, in all cases, counterclaim for infringement. In such cases, the onus is on the proprietor to show that the threats are justified and that the complained of acts constitute infringement. If the plaintiff can prove invalidity or be able to revoke the registration in any relevant respect, then there is an entitlement to the relief sought. However, the mere notification by a registered proprietor that their mark is registered, or that an application for registration has been made, does not constitute a threat.

Therefore, care must be taken when writing 'cease and desist' letters. If the solicitor is sure that the infringing act is one of the three exceptions to the section, then he can make the threat, as the section does not apply. In all other cases, where the section does apply, it is best to merely notify the existence of the registration or application and ask for the acts complained of to cease, without going so far as threatening proceedings.

2.15 Dealings with registered trade marks

For the first time, under s 26 of the 1996 Act, a registered trade mark is statutorily recognised as being personal property. Jointly-owned trademarks cannot be used independently by either of the joint proprietors and in effect the trade mark is treated as if it were registered in a single person's name (s 27 of the 1996 Act).

Just like any other piece of personal property, a registered trade mark can be surrendered, revoked, assigned, charged, willed or transferred by operation of law and can be so dealt with independently of the goodwill of the business in which it is used or with the goodwill of that business (s 28 of the 1996 Act). Furthermore an assignment can be in respect of only some of the goods or services specified in the registration or it can be limited so as to apply to the use of the mark in a particular manner or in a particular locality (s 28(2) of the 1996 Act).

It is very important to remember that any instrument transferring a registered trade mark, be it a deed of assignment or a vesting assent, must be signed in writing by the assignor to be effective (s 23 of the 1996 Act).

Once the registered trade mark has been transferred, application must be made to the Controller of Patents, Designs and Trade Marks to have the particulars of the transaction entered in the register. This requirement to record the transfer applies to:

(a) assignments of a registered trade mark or any right in it;
(b) licences of registered trade marks or an assignment of a licence;
(c) security interests (whether fixed or floating) taken over a registered trade mark or any right in it or under it;
(d) vesting assents by a personal representative in relation to a trade mark or any right in it or under it; or
(e) an order of a court or other competent authority, transferring a registered trade mark or any right accruing to it (s 29(1), (2) of the 1996 Act).

The penalty for ignoring the requirement to record the dealing in the mark is that until the application for recordal of the transfer has been made at the Patents Office the transfer is ineffective as against a third party acquiring a conflicting interest in or under the registered mark in ignorance of the transfer, and, the rights of a licensee under ss 34 or 35 are not operative (s 29(3)(a), (b) of the 1996 Act).

Furthermore, if the application for recordal of the transfer at the Patents Office is not made within six months of the date of the transaction (unless it can be shown that it was not practicable to make the recordal), the person acquiring the registered trade mark will not be entitled to an award of damages or an account of profits in respect of any infringement of the registered trade mark, which occurs after the date of the transaction but before the date that application to record the transaction is actually made at the Patents Office (s 29(4) of the 1996 Act).

Under s 29(5), provision is made for altering (or deleting) the details of transactions already recorded in the Register.

2.16 Licensing

The provisions regarding the licensing of a registered trade mark are to be found in ss 32–36 of the 1996 Act.

Most importantly, it should be noted that a licence may be general in respect of all of the rights accruing to the registered trade marks or limited, for example as to some of the goods or services for which the trade mark is registered or limited as to use of the mark only in a particular manner or in a particular locality (s 32(1), (2) of the 1996 Act). This mirrors the equivalent provisions in respect of trade mark assignments.

Again, like assignments, the licence must be signed by the grantor of the licence to be effective. Furthermore, a licence of a registered trade mark may permit a sublicence to be granted (ss 32(3), (5) of the 1996 Act).

2.17 Exclusive licences

Under ss 33 and 35 of the 1996 Act, rights are given to an exclusive licensee that effectively places them in the place of the trade mark owner. Under s 33(1), such a licence may exclude the registered proprietor himself from any use of the mark during the period of the licence, and under s 35 and 36 an exclusive licensee may, if so entitled, bring infringement proceedings in his own name. However, the right to do this does not supersede or remove the right of the proprietor to sue for infringement, and so the rights of the exclusive licensee in this regard run concurrent with those of the proprietor.

Under s 36, in order to bring infringement proceedings in his sole name, an exclusive licensee must obtain the permission of the court. Otherwise, the exclusive licensee can bring the infringement proceedings, but must join the registered proprietor either as a plaintiff or a defendant, except where an injunction is sought. However, should the registered proprietor be so joined to the action by the exclusive licensee, he will not be liable for any of the costs of the action, unless he actually takes part in the proceedings (s 36(2) of the 1996 Act). In a case where the registered proprietor and exclusive licensee have concurrent rights, the court has a discretion in assessing damages to take account of the terms of the licence and any pecuniary remedy already awarded or available to either of them in respect of the infringement. Furthermore, the court will not grant an account of profits if an award of damages has already been made or an account of profits has been directed in favour of one or other of them in respect of the infringement, the subject of the action. If this is not the case, and the court orders an account of profits, the court has the discretion to apportion the profits between the proprietor and the exclusive licensee as it sees just, subject to any agreement between them on this issue (s 36(3) of the 1996 Act).

Where the registered proprietor and an exclusive licensee have concurrent rights of action, the proprietor must notify the exclusive licensee before applying for a delivery up order under s 20 (s 36(5) of the 1996 Act).

If only one of the exclusive licensee and proprietor is a party to the action, then the court has discretion under s 36(4) to direct that part of any pecuniary award be held on behalf of the non-party.

Finally, s 36(6) provides that these provisions, which govern the exercise of the concurrent rights of a registered proprietor and an exclusive licensee, may be contracted out of by the terms of the exclusive licence.

2.18 Non-exclusive licensees

Section 34 of the 1996 Act sets out the rights of an ordinary general licensee in the case of an infringement. Such a licensee can call on the proprietor of the registered mark to take infringement proceedings and if the proprietor refuses to do so or does not do so within two months of the call, the licensee may bring the proceedings in his own name as if he were the proprietor. As in the case of an exclusive licensee, the general licensee cannot pursue the action in his sole name without the permission of the court. However, he can proceed with the action without the leave of the court, if he joins the proprietor either as plaintiff or defendant to the action.

Again, a general licensee can, without the leave of the court or the joinder of the registered proprietor to the action, pursue an application for an interlocutory injunction. A registered proprietor joined to the action by the licensee will not be liable for the costs of the action, unless he actually takes part in the action. Where an action for infringement is taken by the registered proprietor, the court has discretion to direct a portion of any pecuniary remedy, ie damages awarded to the plaintiff proprietor, to be held on behalf of a licensee whom the court considers has suffered loss or damage.

2.19 Surrender, revocation and invalidity

An important litigation tactic is the ability of the defendant to seek revocation of a registered trade mark or a declaration of invalidity should appropriate grounds for such an application exist.

2.19.1 Surrender

Section 50 of the 1996 Act provides that a trade mark may be surrendered (voluntarily) by the registered proprietor in respect of some or all of the goods or services for which it is registered.

2.19.2 Revocation

Section 51 of the 1996 Act provides that a trade mark must be put to genuine use by the proprietor or with his consent in the State within five years following the date of publication of the registration in relation to the goods or services for which it is registered, unless there are proper reasons for non-use.

Section 51(1)(a) provides that a trade mark may be revoked if no use of the trade mark has occurred. Section 51(1)(b) provides for revocation where use has been made of the mark, but such use has been suspended for an uninterrupted period of five years without proper reason for the suspension of the use.

Section 51(1)(c) provides for revocation of the mark in circumstances where it has become a common name (ie, generic) in the trade for a product or service for which it is registered (see my earlier discussion of generic trade marks).

Finally, s 51(1)(d) provides for revocation where a trademark has, because of the use made of it, become liable to mislead the public in relation to the goods or services for which it is registered, eg, in regard to the nature of those goods or services, their quality or geographical origin.

An example might be a dairy product entitled 'Devon's Best' registered for cream. If this is used in relation to a synthetic cream or if it is used for a cream which is produced in Wexford, the mark may be liable as deceptive as to: (a) quality; and (b) geographical origin, because the public would expect the product to be clotted cream or at least genuine full cream and produced in Devon.

When revocation proceedings are instituted, pursuant to s 51(3), the period of three months before the application is filed is disregarded, unless preparations for the commencement or resumption of the use of the mark began before the proprietor became aware that the application might be made.

It should be noted that under the Act, revocation proceedings can be instituted by any person and the onus to prove 'use' lies with the trade mark proprietor (s 99 of the 1996 Act). An application for revocation can be made either to the Controller of Patents, Designs and Trade Marks in the Patents Office or to the court (namely the High Court), except where proceedings (eg, infringement proceedings) concerning the trade mark are already pending in the High Court, in which case the application must be made to the High Court rather than to the Controller. In practice, where there are valid grounds, an application for revocation is usually made as a counterclaim to an action for infringement and is a very useful strategy.

As in the circumstances of surrendering, revocation can be in respect of some of the goods or services for which the mark is registered. In the general commercial environment, trade marks do not remain stagnant and are amended and altered over time. This is recognised in s 51, which states that use of the mark will include use in a form differing in elements which do not alter the distinctive character of the mark in the form in which it was registered. 'Use' for the purposes of the provision will be deemed to include the fixing of the mark to the goods or to the packaging of goods in the State solely for export.

If revocation proceedings are successful before the Controller of the Patents Office, the registration in question will be revoked and the rights of the proprietor deemed to have ceased as and from the date of the application for revocation or if the Controller is satisfied that the grounds for revocation existed at an earlier date, that date will be applied.

2.19.3 Invalidity

Another key line of defence in infringement proceedings is the ability to contest the registration on the basis that it is invalid. The grounds for invalidity are set out in s 52 of the 1996 Act. The invalidity may be claimed on the basis that the mark was registered in contravention of the 'absolute' grounds in s 8 for refusal for registration. However, the mark will not be held to be invalid if the claim is one where invalidity is asserted, because the mark is alleged to contravene s 8(1)(b), (c) or (d) but where the owner can show that by virtue of use since registration, the mark has now become distinctive. The grounds in the subsections are that the mark at the time of registration should not have been registered, because it lacked distinctiveness, was a purely descriptive term or sign, or was a generic term in the trade in which the mark was to be used.

Furthermore, under s 52, invalidity may be claimed on the basis of contravention of the 'relative' grounds for refusal as conflicting with earlier rights, unless the proprietor of earlier trade marks consented to the registration.

Again, there is discretion as to whether the application for a declaration of invalidity be made to the Controller or to the court but again, the application must be made to the court where there are existing proceedings pending in relation to the same trade mark in the court.

A further ground for claiming invalidity is that the registration of the mark was made in bad faith.

As in the case of revocation, the mark may be declared invalid in respect of only some of the goods or services for which it's registered. Where a mark has been deemed to be invalid to any extent, the registration shall, to that extent, be deemed never to have been made, providing that the declaration of invalidity will not affect transactions past and closed (s 52(4), (5) and (6) of the 1996 Act).

Invalidity may be built on conflict with earlier rights but if the proprietor of the earlier conflicting trade mark, being aware of the use of the registered trade mark in the State, has acquiesced to that use for a period of five years, that proprietor of the earlier trade mark loses the right to apply for a declaration that the registration of the later trade mark is invalid or to oppose the use of the later registered trade mark unless the registration of the later registered trade mark was applied for in bad faith. However, equally, the proprietor of the later registered trade mark cannot oppose the use of the earlier trade mark (s 53 of the 1996 Act).

Finally, on the subject of invalidity, pursuant to s 76, the registration of the trade mark is *prima facie* evidence of the validity of the original registration and of any transactions such as assignments concerning it. In other words, there is a presumption of validity in favour of the registered proprietor.

2.20 Collective mark and certification mark

The Trade Marks Act 1996 makes provision for the registration of two unusual genres of marks, namely:

(a) under s 54(1), a 'collective mark', which is a mark distinguishing the goods or services of members of the association which is the proprietor of the mark from those of other undertakings, may be registered (and the provisions dealing with collective marks are contained in Sched 1 to the 1996 Act);

(b) under s 55(1), a 'certification mark', which is a mark indicating that the goods or services in connection with which the mark is used are certified by the proprietor of that mark in respect of origin, material, mode of manufacture of goods or performance of services, quality, accuracy or other characteristics (and the provisions dealing with certification marks are contained in Sched 2 to the 1996 Act).

Both these categories of marks are governed by regulations, which in the case of collective marks must be approved by the Controller and in the case of certification marks must be approved by the Minister for Enterprise, Trade and Employment. Once approval has been granted, the normal steps for registration are completed.

2.21 Famous marks

Under s 61 of the 1996 Act, a 'well-known' trade mark is defined as one which is well-known in this state as being the mark belonging to a national of a member country to the Paris Convention or domiciled or operating commercially in a Convention country.

Such a well-known mark need not be in use in Ireland. In other words, this refers to marks which are well-known in Ireland but which are not necessarily used in trade in Ireland. Two examples which spring to mind are 'GAP' and 'IKEA' which are not in commercial use here, but which are almost household names. Under s 61(2), the proprietor of such a 'well-known' mark is entitled to restrain by injunction the use of the famous mark in Ireland.

2.22 Offences

The 1996 Act introduced, for the first time, offences for the fraudulent application or use of a registered trade mark. Section 92(1) of the 1996 Act sets out a list of acts which if done in relation to a registered trade mark will constitute an offence but s 92(3) adds the proviso that an offence will only be committed if the acts are committed with a 'view to gain' or 'with intent to cause a loss to another'.

This subsection also provides that there is a defence to the charge if the person charged can establish that he believed on reasonable grounds that he was entitled to use the trade mark in relation to the goods in question. The penalties for the commission of such an offence are:

(a) on summary conviction – up to six months' imprisonment or a fine of up to €1,269.74 or both;

(b) on indictment – up to five years' imprisonment or a fine of up to €126,973.80 or both.

Other offences are falsification of the Trade Marks Register (s 93 of the 1996 Act) or falsely representing a mark as registered (s 94 of the 1996 Act).

2.23 Jurisdiction

While in general, the High Court has jurisdiction in regard to matters arising under the Act, it should be noted that s 96 of the 1996 Act confers jurisdiction on the local circuit court to make an order for delivery up under s 20 and for destructive or forfeiture of infringing goods under s 23.

2.24 Community trade mark (CTM)

Finally, the CTM and important provisions relating to it are set out below.

2.24.1 Duration

As mentioned above, the duration of a CTM is the same as a national registration and like a national mark it can be licensed, assigned, revoked, surrendered or invalidated.

2.24.2 Infringement

A CTM registration gives the registered owner the exclusive right to prevent others from using, in the course of trade, a mark that is identical or confusingly similar to that registered.

The provisions of Art 9 of the Regulation (see section 2.4.2 above) are identical to the provisions of s 14 of the 1996 Act. Once the provisions of Art 9 are satisfied, infringement will be deemed to arise.

However, registration of a CTM does not entitle the proprietor to prohibit the use of that mark in relation to goods which are put on the market in the Community by the proprietor or with their consent. The principle of 'exhaustion of rights' will not apply in circumstances where there is a legitimate reason to oppose the further commercialisation of the goods.

2.24.3 Jurisdiction

If infringement has occurred, where should the proceedings be instituted? It should first be noted that the Regulation did not set up a special court to deal with CTM issues such as infringement, invalidity and revocation. Instead, each Member State was asked to designate a court in their own jurisdiction to handle such matters. The court nominated by the Irish Government is the High Court.

The jurisdiction selected by a litigant is governed by the following rules as set down in Art 93:

(a) proceedings are brought in the courts of the Member State in which the defendant is domiciled;

(b) if the defendant is not domiciled in any Member State, the proceedings are brought in the Member State in which the defendant has an establishment;
(c) if the defendant is not domiciled nor established in any Member State, the proceedings are brought in the Member State in which the plaintiff is domiciled;
(d) if the plaintiff is not domiciled in any Member State, the proceedings are brought in the Member State in which the plaintiff has an establishment;
(e) if neither the defendant nor the plaintiff are domiciled or have an establishment in any Member State, proceedings are brought in the Spanish courts.

It is assumed that 'establishment' means 'a real and effective establishment' in the territory of one of the countries of the European Union.

Despite the above stringent conditions, there are two other circumstances in which a CTM court can be given exclusive jurisdiction which are:

(a) where the parties agree that a different CTM court will hear the dispute;
(b) where the defendant enters an appearance before a different CTM court.

The final choice of jurisdiction permits actions to be brought before the CTM court of the Member State where the act of infringement was committed. However, the court's jurisdiction relates only to acts of infringement committed or threatened within that Member State or acts of infringement committed between the date of publication of the application and the date of publication of registration within that Member State.

2.24.4 Remedies

When infringement has been deemed by the court to have occurred, it shall issue an order prohibiting the defendant from continuing with the conduct and apply the laws of the Member State ranging from damages or on account of profits to delivery up and destruction of infringing goods. Interim relief such as provisional and protective measures can also be granted.

2.24.5 Acquiescence

As with an Irish trade mark, if the proprietor of a CTM acquiesces for five years to the use of a later CTM, they cannot apply for a declaration that the later mark is invalid and from opposing the use of that mark unless the registration of that mark was made in bad faith.

2.24.6 Seniority

Where a CTM proprietor is the owner of an earlier national registration for an identical mark and goods or services, a claim for seniority can be made. By doing so, it means that if the proprietor fails to renew the national registration, he will continue to have the same rights as he would have had if the earlier national registration had been retained.

CHAPTER 3

THE LAW OF PASSING OFF

James Murray

3.1 Introduction

This chapter seeks to provide a practical introduction to the law of passing off. Many of those reading this will have studied intellectual property law as part of their legal studies, and will be familiar with passing off as one of the core 'areas' of intellectual property law. That said, it is often the case that passing off constitutes an area tucked away at the end of the text books or series of lectures, after one has dealt with what are seen as the key areas of patents, copyright and trade marks. Indeed, in intellectual property litigation, passing off is often somewhat of an afterthought, shoved into a plenary summons to ensure that absolutely everything is covered and often not pursued in subsequent proceedings. This chapter, in addition to restating the core elements of a passing off action, also seeks to outline the practical uses of this common law remedy, and to suggest how in practice one might both recognise and deal with such a claim.

3.2 Core principles

What exactly is passing off? Passing off is part of the law of tort and therefore founded in common law, based purely on case law and without any statutory basis in legislation or statutory instrument. Effectively, it seeks to protect the rights of an individual or business, by protecting the goodwill of that business from unfair trading by other parties. This is achieved by preventing other parties from carrying on business or from selling their products under a name, mark, description or in any other manner which could mislead the public (in the sense of the likely market for that business or product) by confusing them to believe that the business or goods in question are those of the plaintiff. In this way, businesses who have invested considerable time, effort and resources in creating a reputation in a particular product or service (but who cannot or have not, for whatever reason, any protection from the law of trade marks) are allowed to protect their investment. Some see passing off as the poor relation of trade mark law, and something to be used only when one does not enjoy trade mark rights. Certainly, trade mark rights constitute a monopoly right, which can often be easier to assert by reliance on the trade mark register, but passing off has its own advantages and variations and has evolved in recent years to offer protection in a wider range of areas than might ever have been envisaged some decades back. These include the twin areas of character merchandising and personality rights, and some have even touted it as forming the basis of a new tort of unfair competition.

Being a tort, one is forced to trawl through a considerable body of case law, primarily English, but also some more recent Irish case law, to extract a working definition of the tort, which allows one to understand and examine the various concepts which go to make up passing off. Each practitioner has his own preferred case which sets the elements of passing off. Here, the case of *Ervin Warnink BV v J Townsend and Sons (Hull) Ltd* [1979] AC 731, a case commonly called the *Advocaat* case, is used. In that case, Lord Diplock set out the five elements which must be present in a given set of circumstances to create a successful cause of action for passing off:

There must be a:

(a) misrepresentation;
(b) made by a trader in the course of trade;
(c) to prospective customers of his (or ultimate consumers of goods or services supplied by him);
(d) which is calculated to injure the business or goodwill of another trader;
(e) which causes actual damage to a business or goodwill of the trader by whom the action is brought (or will probably do so).

The only way to properly understand how to assess whether or not a case of passing off exists is to examine each of these five elements in turn, and discuss briefly the case law pertaining to each of these elements. Such a step by step approach should be used also by practitioners to assess, when approached by a client, whether or not passing off constitutes a reasonable plea. What then of the individual five elements?

3.3 Misrepresentation

Misrepresentation in itself constitutes a core action in tort law, and all practising lawyers come across misrepresentation in a wide variety of situations in their litigation case load. There is no great novelty to the definition of misrepresentation in the context of passing off. The vital thing to bear in mind is that any false representation made by the defendant seeking to create, in the mind of the public or consumers, an unwarranted association with another person (the plaintiff), can be actionable in passing off if there is a real risk of damage occurring to the plaintiff. A useful example of this is the case of *An Post and Others v Irish Permanent* [1995] IR 140, where the defendants launched a new product known as 'Savings Certificates' in July 1994, in circumstances where the plaintiffs had been involved for 65 years in the promotion and sale of a financial savings product under the name 'Savings Certificates' (and where evidence was produced that some IR£3 billion of savings certificates had been sold by An Post in the previous three years). The plaintiffs in that case successfully obtained an interlocutory injunction, despite the defendants' case that the words 'Savings Certificates' were a generic or descriptive name in which the plaintiffs enjoyed no rights. The High Court ruled that there was a case to answer in relation to the allegation that the defendants were seeking to unfairly take advantage of the considerable reputation built up over many decades by the plaintiffs. The misrepresentation in question was found to be material as the court found it could have a direct effect on sales of the defendants' 'Savings Certificates' products.

There are numerous examples, even in Irish case law, illustrating the issue of misrepresentation in so called 'copycat' or 'lookalike' cases. One such case is that of *Gabicci plc v Dunnes Stores* (High Court, 1991, unreported, Carroll J), where the plaintiff successfully obtained an injunction against Dunnes Stores preventing the sale of jumpers, which, it was alleged, were a direct imitation of designs from the 'M range' made popular by the plaintiffs, but sold by Dunnes Stores at half the price. Ms Justice Carroll herself stated that it was extremely difficult to tell the two jumpers apart, and matters were further complicated by the fact that Dunnes Stores' jumpers were made by the Italian factory which also manufactured the Gabicci product. She said:

This is not a case of Dunnes following a fashion trend and giving good value. It concerns the sale of sweaters which, to all intents and purposes, are 'the plaintiff's sweaters' and which it is alleged has created confusion to the public, with resultant damage to the plaintiff's goodwill.

The 1995 case of *B & S Ltd v Irish Autotrader Ltd* [1995] IR 142 (the *Buy and Sell* case) is an example, however, of refusal of an interlocutory injunction. The plaintiff company was the publisher of the well-known magazine, '*Buy and Sell*'. That magazine, circulating mainly in the Republic of Ireland, included advertisements for motor vehicles and accessories and, since February 1994, had carried the words 'including Autotrader' on the cover page of the magazine, with the heading 'Autotrader' also appearing over the motor section. The defendant company had, for the previous 10 years, published in the UK a magazine under the name 'Auto Trader' devoted purely to advertising motor vehicles and accessories, and in February 1995 it launched a magazine, intended to have an all-Ireland readership, dedicated to advertisements for motor vehicles and accessories, called 'Irish Auto Trader'. However, Mr Justice McCracken refused to grant the interlocutory application on the basis of the balance of convenience, finding that the possible loss to the defendant, by either preventing distribution of the magazine in Ireland or forcing them to change the name, would considerably exceed the possible loss to the plaintiff. He was clearly influenced by the fact that the bulk of advertising in both magazines (and upon which both publications heavily relied) came from traders, whom the court felt would not be easily confused between the two magazines when choosing where to advertise.

In the 1996 case of *R Griggs Group Ltd and Others v Dunnes Stores* (High Court, 1996, unreported, Dublin, McCracken J), the court also refused to grant the plaintiff an interlocutory injunction. The plaintiff company was the manufacturer of the famous Doc Martens footwear, while Dunnes Stores was selling children's boots that were practically identical to the plaintiffs' products (although cheaper). Dunnes Stores had also labelled the boots as 'Docs', the name by which the authentic footwear had been colloquially known for many years. Despite the facts, the court refused to grant the interlocutory injunction on the basis that the plaintiffs were a worldwide company which would suffer minimal damage between the hearing of the interlocutory injunction and the plenary hearing, whereas the likely loss to Dunnes Stores arising from an injunction would be much greater. It was on this basis, that of the balance of convenience, that the court refused to grant the injunction. This decision was criticised by some commentators as taking an unduly generous approach towards lookalike products, but the court may have been influenced in those circumstances by certain undertakings provided to the court by the defendants which lessened the likelihood of damage being suffered by the plaintiffs prior to plenary hearing.

A rare Supreme Court decision in relation to passing off, some years earlier, was the case of *adidas v Charles O'Neill and Co Ltd* [1983] ILRM 112. That case concerned the distinctiveness of a three-stripe design on sportswear. The evidence was that in 1967 the world-famous adidas company commenced manufacture of sportswear, such as tracksuits, which had a distinctive three-stripe design down the sides of the arms and legs of the tracksuits and jerseys. In 1976, adidas commenced manufacturing their sports gear in Ireland, thereby coming into direct competition with O'Neill and Co, which was by then long established in the Irish sports market. The evidence was that in 1965, O'Neill's started putting stripes on its products, initially varying between one and three stripes, but within a few years concentrating on a three-stripe design. Evidence at the trial alleged that the three-stripe design had been used by manufacturers of sportswear in many countries, but that adidas was the only manufacturer who exclusively used the particular arrangement of light-coloured stripes of equal width, set against a differently coloured background. It was therefore claimed that O'Neill's, by using a three-stripe design, was passing off its products as those of adidas. The defendant company claimed that the adidas three-stripe design was not part of adidas' goodwill and that the plaintiff company could not prove that it had an exclusive association with that design on products in Ireland. The High Court refused to grant relief, and this was upheld by the Supreme Court, who stated that the use of the stripes of varying colours and numbers on sports garments was a fashion in the trade and that O'Neill's, in resorting to fashionable demands, had not attempted to deceive or pass off, and in fact had not done so. The court stated that:

> The mere copying of a design or the anticipation of a fashion, or the taking advantage of a market or demand created by another's advertising, is not of itself sufficient to support an action for passing off if the trader against whom the complaint is made has sufficiently distinguished his goods so that confusion is not created.

There is much case law on this point, but, unfortunately for the purposes of elucidating legal principles, the majority of it concludes at the interlocutory injunction phase (following which most parties appear to either reach settlement or simply decline to proceed with the action to plenary hearing). However, the above case law provides a useful snapshot of the types of misrepresentations which are potentially actionable under the law of passing off. It is worth stating at this point that it is not absolutely essential that the defendant and plaintiff operate in precisely the same field, so long as it can be demonstrated that the plaintiff has a reputation which could potentially be affected by the defendant taking business advantage of that reputation.

3.4 Made by a trader in the course of trade

The 'made by a trader in the course of trade' requirement is relatively self-explanatory and, indeed, to a large extent is superfluous, as a plaintiff who is not trading will presumably not be able to demonstrate damage to his business or goodwill (and thereby not meet part (e) of the requirements). There is little to note in the case law regarding this requirement, and certainly Irish courts do not appear to have made an issue of it at any time. It appears that anyone who makes an income from the provision of goods or services can qualify as a trader, and the range of organisations which have been able to pursue actions in passing off include the British Medical Association, the BBC and Dr Barnardo's, although it has also been found by UK courts that a political party could not qualify as a trader on the basis that its involvement was not in commercial activity. In the majority of cases, however, this will not be a real concern for the legal practitioner.

3.5 To prospective customers

In many cases, the plaintiffs will seek to adduce evidence from actual or potential customers regarding actual confusion allegedly arising from the representation made by the defendant. This can take the form of personal evidence or survey evidence. The purpose of introducing such evidence is to forcefully demonstrate to the court the impact of the misrepresentation on the business or goodwill of the plaintiff. It can be useful, from a practical point of view, if the plaintiff can show real life examples of either confusion or deception on the part of a customer when faced with the defendant's product or service. That said, it is ultimately a matter for the judge hearing the case as to whether or not he is convinced that a reasonable man or, indeed, a reasonable purchaser, could be confused by the existence of the defendant's product or business.

A good illustration of this is the case of *Symonds Cider and Others v Showerings (Ireland) Ltd* [1997] 1 ILRM 482 (the *Symonds* case). That case concerned 'Scrumpy Jack' cider imported into Ireland and a rival product known as 'Golden Scrumpy'. In refusing to grant the injunction sought in those proceedings, Ms Justice Carroll also made clear that she was not having any regard to the market research evidence submitted by the parties in relation to the likelihood of confusion. She said:

> I believe that my experience as an ordinary shopper or consumer enables me, just as well as any other, to assess the likelihood of confusion.

Indeed, she clearly felt that it was more appropriate for the court to make this decision without, perhaps, being manipulated by the evidence of either party on this point. In an Irish court, the reasonable man, or the prospective customer of the plaintiff, is a test which ultimately falls to be considered by the judge hearing the case.

3.6 Business or goodwill

The business or goodwill element would again seem to be self-explanatory, and all lawyers will know what is meant by business or goodwill in the normal sense of those words. However, the meaning of goodwill in the context of passing off actions has shifted somewhat in recent years. It remains clear that the plaintiff must satisfy the court that the business affected by the alleged passing off has been trading for some time and has built up goodwill within the jurisdiction in that product or business. An important Irish case is *C & A Modes Ltd v C & A Waterford Ltd* [1978] SSR 126. In that case, the court accepted that even though the plaintiff, a group of chain stores with branches throughout Europe, had no store in the Republic of Ireland, there was regular custom from this jurisdiction to the C & A store in Belfast, and exposure in the Republic of Ireland to C & A Modes' advertising in various British publications and British television circulating within this jurisdiction. Therefore, although not actually trading within the jurisdiction, foreign trading in a context which created considerable public exposure in the jurisdiction was sufficient to fulfil this element of passing off.

Another Irish case worth noting is *O'Neill's Irish International Sports Co Ltd and Others v O'Neill's Footwear Dryer Co Ltd* (High Court, 30 April 1997, unreported, Barron J). The defendant company, owned by a Mr John O'Neill, had succeeded in obtaining a patent for an electronically operated shoe dryer, but he could not find any financial support from sports manufacturers (including the plaintiffs) to enable him to manufacture it himself. He therefore imported a similar product from the Far East and sold it in a box similar to a shoe box, with the box label referring variously to an O'Neill's footwear dryer, Celbridge, Ireland, and 'Made in China'. The plaintiff (the company that was the defendant in the adidas case discussed above) sought an injunction on the basis of passing off, claiming that the defendant was trading on the reputation which they had built up in the name O'Neill's, and despite the plaintiff's own surname, the court agreed with this. Having reviewed the authorities, the court was satisfied:

> ... that the defendant had presented its goods to the public in such a manner as to be able to take advantage of the reputation and goodwill generated by the plaintiffs.

The court clearly felt that the manner in which the product was marketed, together with using the word 'O'Neill's', constituted an effort to obtain deliberate advantage – due simply to the pre-existing reputation of the O'Neill's brand in a parallel market.

A more recent case is *Guinness Ireland and Others v Kilkenny Brewing Co Ltd* [1999] ILRM 531. The world-famous plaintiff company marketed, *inter alia*, Kilkenny Irish Beer, while the defendant company was incorporated in 1995 with a view to carrying on the business of brewing and marketing beers. The plaintiff claimed an exclusive reputation in the use of the name 'Kilkenny' in connection with beer, alleging that consumers could be confused or deceived into perceiving an association between the defendant and Guinness. Miss Justice Laffoy granted an injunction stating that:

(a) passing off included the incorporation of a company with a name likely to give an impression to the public that it is associated or connected with another company – whether the impugned name was intentionally or innocently chosen was irrelevant;

(b) by December 1995 (the date of incorporation of the defendant), the plaintiff had an established goodwill in the name Kilkenny when used with beer (mainly through the product known as 'Kilkenny'), and there was a real likelihood that the public would get an impression of a connection between the two businesses;

(c) the fact that the defendant intended to act as a land holding company, not as a trading company, did not immure its choice of name from public perception.

A further point to be made, which will perhaps have become clear from the case law mentioned, is that the conduct need not be 'calculated' in the sense that one might ordinarily use that word. It is enough that the effect of the conduct is to create a situation of passing off, and the question of whether or not the conduct was deliberate is not crucial either way. What is crucial is that confusion has arisen with resulting damage to the plaintiff.

3.7 Damage

Obviously, a key element in any successful tort action is demonstrating that the defendant's actions caused or are likely to cause damage to the plaintiff. Where the plaintiff has already suffered damage, in the sense that it can be shown that the public is confused as to ownership of products or services, with resultant damage to the plaintiff's goodwill and/or reputation, this is not a difficult element to prove. However, the vast majority of passing off actions which come to court arise at the interlocutory injunction stage, where it is likely that the plaintiff is attempting to pre-empt the establishment of a reputation by the defendant, and therefore the defendant will (hopefully) have had little opportunity to cause damage. However, in practice, once goodwill and reputation are shown, it is generally not difficult to demonstrate that damage is likely to occur.

The leading Irish case to examine the question of damage is *Falcon Travel Ltd v Falcon Leisure Group* [1991] IR 175. In that case, the plaintiff was a travel agency operating in Dublin and Wicklow since 1970, with a significant reputation in the retail travel agent business. The defendant was a major tour operator in the UK since the early 1980s, primarily operating as a wholesaler selling its products to travel agents, such as the plaintiff. However, in 1988, it launched a brochure directed exclusively to the Irish market, and opened an office in Ireland. The evidence was that, while aware of the existence of the plaintiff, it did not anticipate any confusion between them because of the differences in their areas of operation. While there had been some initial confusion following the direct entry of Falcon Leisure into the Irish market, those instances of confusion had diminished significantly to the date of the action in 1990. The judge accepted that there was no fraud or deceit involved, and that the defendant did not intend or expect to expropriate the reputation of the plaintiff or any part of the business of the plaintiff. The plaintiff had not lost any customers to the defendant, but its main complaint was the fear that people would think it was the defendant. The defendant asserted that as a matter of law, the plaintiff could not succeed in an action for passing off, unless it established that the action complained of not merely gave rise to confusion, but confusion which caused damage, or at least the real likelihood of damage. However, Mr Justice Murphy granted the plaintiff damages, while stating the following:

(a) that it is possible to establish measurable and observable damage in many actions of passing off which was a consequence of a defendant's wrongful appropriation of the plaintiff's goodwill;

(b) that in a passing off action, it was the appropriation of the goodwill *in itself* which constituted the damage required and not the consequences of appropriation, such as loss of business (emphasis added). The tort was complete when the reputation was appropriated;

(c) that the plaintiff was entitled to succeed because its goodwill had become submerged in that of the defendant, as a direct result of the defendant's actions.

The court then took the unusual step of not granting an injunction to the plaintiff, but instead awarding damages to ensure that the plaintiff could launch an advertising campaign, which would ensure that the public was aware of the difference between the plaintiff and the defendant.

This case is an unusual example of the fifth element of the passing off action. Generally, it will be clear whether or not the plaintiff is likely to suffer damage resulting from the action of the defendant and, more likely than not, that damage will be financial resulting from lost sales or potential loss of goodwill or reputation. The court, when requested, and on finding that there is a case of passing off, is likely to grant interlocutory relief. Many cases will concern start-up or relatively new businesses as defendants, and the granting of such relief is seen as the surest way to protect the reputation of plaintiffs from such attack.

That is a brief summary of the five crucial elements required to found an action for passing off. Some of the case law uses a three-pronged test, while others use a five-pronged test (as in section 3.2 above), but all of the elements mentioned above will have to be satisfied at the end of the day. Hopefully the gist of the action of passing off will now be clear and the reader will be in a position to recognise when it might be an appropriate plea to raise (whether that be in plenary proceedings or as part of an interlocutory application). It goes without saying that there is often a high level of subjectivity in assessing whether or not a plaintiff has a good case in passing off. It can often be extremely difficult to ascertain whether or not passing off is present, and many situations where this tort is alleged are borderline. Lawyers practising in the area of passing off realise that passing off can be alleged in relation to absolutely any good or service which is being traded. One must consider all the circumstances of the case, and remember that the ultimate test is that of the reasonable purchaser who might wish to purchase the plaintiff's product.

That purchaser may know much more about the nature and qualities of the product in question than Joe Bloggs off the number 10 bus, a point illustrated by the decision in the *Buy and Sell* case (cited in section 3.3 above). That purchaser must be confused into thinking that he is buying either the plaintiff's products/services or products/services associated with the plaintiff. It is not enough in most cases to show that the consumer thinks this is a good enough imitation, at a cheaper price, to satisfy his needs.

This, to an extent, is illustrated by the attitude of Ms Justice Carroll in the *Symonds* case (cited in section 3.5 above) which illustrates that the court will make the decision whether or not the reasonable consumer would be confused by the parallel goods or services in question. Confusion, or even deceit, is inherently subjective, and what might confuse one individual on a given day in a particular set of circumstances might not confuse another individual. In addition, it must be remembered that the context in which the tort of passing off is set is an ever-changing one. Consumer awareness and brand awareness shift on a regular basis and, for example, many would submit that anyone buying a Manchester United shirt on Talbot Street for €5 is certainly not under the impression that he is buying the real thing, and therefore a crucial element is missing in order to satisfy a passing off action. Such circumstances may, of course, give rise to alternative legal remedies. In relation to counterfeit goods and the particular statutory regime governing the area, one should bear in mind the potential overlap with the law of passing off in such cases.

3.8 The evolution of passing off: character merchandising

To an extent, the tort of passing off has taken a new lease of life within the past decade or so, due to the ever-changing nature of merchandising goods and the ever-heightening awareness of the value of brand awareness in today's market place. Passing off has been used to underpin the protection of so-called 'character merchandising', and the law in this area is generally taken to derive from the New South Wales case of *Children's Television Workshop Inc v Woolworths (New South Wales) Ltd* [1981] RPC 187 (the *Muppets* case). Woolworths was selling unlicensed products of Muppet characters from Sesame Street, whose popularity in Australia at the time was demonstrated by the fact that many millions of Australian dollars per annum were being spent on licensed Sesame Street merchandise. The plaintiffs did not actually produce the Sesame Street merchandise themselves, but rather licensed their rights to third parties, but the court felt that the public of 1981 would be aware of the practice of character merchandising, and that their reputation and goodwill would thereby suffer by the fact that the Woolworths toys were cheaper and of inferior quality to the licensed products. Since then, courts in Australia, and also in the US, have used the tort of passing off to protect the licensing practices of parties, such as the plaintiffs in the *Muppets* case, to cover Teenage Mutant Ninja Turtles, Crocodile Dundee imitations in television advertisements and other products of character merchandising.

3.9 Personality rights

The courts in England have been less ready to protect such rights, and the Spice Girls famously failed to obtain an injunction against an Italian company which used photographs of them as collectable stickers on their products. As yet, the Irish courts have failed to protect character merchandising using passing off, but nevertheless an Irish court might well be prepared to grant an injunction in such circumstances. The only reported case, and that was only a newspaper report, was an action taken in 2001 by Olympic gold medallist Mary Peters against Ark Life Assurance Company. She alleged that by using her image in an advertising campaign, which recalled key events of various years (including 1972, the year in which Ms Peters won Olympic gold), it was creating the impression that she had agreed to do this. Crucially, she also claimed that inclusion in the Ark Life ads precluded her from doing business with other Irish financial institutions, and she claimed that she had intended to exploit her image in the future. The case was settled out of court, supposedly for a 'substantial five-figure sum'.

An important development is the 2001 English case of *Irvine v Talksport Ltd* [2002] 2 All ER 214, a case involving the well-known racing driver, Eddie Irvine. The defendant radio station had acquired, from an agency, a photograph of Irvine using a mobile telephone and had manipulated that photograph to give the appearance that he was in fact listening to a radio. The photograph was subsequently circulated on brochures for the defendant radio station (which specialised in coverage of sporting events), and Irvine claimed that the use of his photograph in such circumstances amounted to a misrepresentation that he endorsed the defendant's programme. The question therefore was whether a false representation of endorsement could amount to a passing off, and Mr Justice Laddie of the English High Court found that it could. He stated as follows:

> Large sums are paid for endorsement ... because ... those in business have reason to believe that the lustre of a famous personality, if attached to their goods or services, will enhance the attractiveness of those goods or services to their target market.

The court explicitly found that exploitation of a famous personality's goodwill can be distinguished from mere merchandising, and therefore that passing off can be used to prevent unlicensed use of goodwill, which could reduce, blur or diminish its exclusivity. Importantly, the court said that an underlying principle of the tort of passing off was the 'maintenance of what is currently regarded as fair trading', and approved the evolution of the passing off action from very narrow parameters, to the extent of what is envisaged by the *Irvine* case. The court ruled that such a case could succeed where the plaintiff could first show that he has a significant reputation or goodwill to protect and, secondly, that the actions of the defendant communicated a 'false message' that the plaintiff endorsed or approved the goods or services provided by the defendant.

It is submitted that this decision by the most eminent intellectual property lawyer on the English Bench is likely to be influential in the event that a similar case comes before the Irish courts. There is the potential additional factor in Ireland, mentioned in some of the intellectual property commentaries, that the State is constitutionally obliged to protect the property rights of all its citizens, although this protection in itself has not been explored to the fullest. Character merchandising is not confined, of course, to cartoon characters, such as Barbie or Barney, or whatever the children's favourite at the time might be. There is also the question of whether or not, for example, famous footballers could utilise the tort of passing off to assert so-called 'personality rights' to prevent a third party unfairly taking advantage of their reputation. Some decades back, the argument might have been that a footballer was a public figure and, particularly when the game was amateur, that there was no reason not to use the names of prominent individuals when promoting a product. With evolution of the market in recent years, many footballers, musicians and others derive a considerable part of their income from exploitation of the value apparently to be gained by endorsement of specific products. More importantly, consumers are more aware of this practice and seem to attach far more importance to whether something is for example an 'authorised' product or 'recommended' by a particular personality. While originally individuals were only able to protect their rights in this regard by use of the breach of confidence action together with some kind of muddled (though never explicitly stated) right to privacy, there appears to be no specific reason why such individuals cannot now satisfy all the elements of the passing off action where a third party seeks to use their image or name to protect a particular product. It may not be long before an Irish court is asked to adjudicate on this area and the role of the tort of passing off in protecting such putative rights.

3.10 Practical steps in dealing with passing off

This chapter concludes with some practical advice for those legal advisers who find that they have successfully identified that there is indeed a passing off element arising in their client's case, whether it be as plaintiff or defendant. What should they do? What must they avoid? A key point to remember is that the vast majority of passing off actions which come to court are decided at the interlocutory injunction stage. Following an injunction ruling, parties almost invariably work things out between themselves rather than face a long and expensive road to plenary hearing. The success or failure of an attempt to obtain interlocutory relief is crucial in determining whether or not the goods or services which are alleged to be passing off will have anything other than a very short lifespan. Therefore, when confronted with facts which alert one to the existence of a passing off action, think in terms of the proofs required to satisfy the granting of an interim or interlocutory injunction, as well as the five elements set out in this chapter to succeed at passing off.

As a plaintiff, one needs to move quickly as any delay in taking action against the alleged offender will be viewed harshly by the court. Delay is the death knell for many would-be interlocutory applications. Remember that failure to succeed in progressing the matter to an interlocutory hearing within a short period of time could, in some circumstances, give rise to the prospect of a defendant who, two years down the line, has built up his own reputation in a particular product and will not be found by a court to be a parasite on another person's reputation.

Immediately on being made aware that there is a case which sounds like it might fall within the parameters of passing off, comprehensive instructions should be taken in order to draft a 'cease and desist' letter. That letter should contain as much information as possible about what your client knows of the nature of the potential infringement, when and where it has taken place and should issue an ultimatum to the potential defendant to cease the offending action. Remember that this letter could be the foundation of an interim or interlocutory application, and it should seek to deal with all of the defendant's activities (including marketing activities which could offend a client's rights). One caveat here is that such a letter should not fall foul of the provisions in trade mark law (see Chapter 2 ante), which deal with groundless threats of trade mark infringement. Failing a response from the defendant, or at least failing a response which adequately meets a plaintiff's demands, Counsel should be briefed immediately (having considered the existence or otherwise of the five elements named above), with a view to instituting proceedings. One cannot emphasise enough that the approach to a passing off case must display a level of urgency that, for example, would not be present in a typical personal injuries case. Once Counsel has been briefed, he can advise on the necessary proofs in order to proceed to enforce a client's rights. Crucial to this, as we have already seen, will be evidence of existing reputation and goodwill, and evidence of confusion on the part of existing or potential customers. For example, one may need to assemble all evidence of a client's marketing activities over previous years, together with evidence regarding volume of sales and any other impact in the market place. The key thing to remember in passing off is to move quickly, because delay may be fatal to the protection of valuable intellectual property rights.

CHAPTER 4

PATENTS

Ken Parkinson and Andrew Parkes

4.1 Patent law

A patent is a monopoly granted by the State in respect of an invention as an incentive to innovate.

Patent law is the creature of statute. Prior to the foundation of the Irish State, UK statutes applied. Since the foundation of the Irish State, three Acts dealing with patents have been enacted. First, the Industrial and Commercial Property (Protection) Act 1927; secondly the Patents Act 1964, which repealed the patent provisions of the 1927 Act; and, finally, the Patents Act 1992 (PA92) which repealed the 1964 Act.

The 1992 Act is implemented by the Patents Rules 1992 (PR92) (SI 1992/172), with the current fees being laid down in the Patents, Trade Marks and Designs (Fees) Rules 2001 (SI 2001/482). Other relevant secondary legislation includes the European Communities (Supplementary Protection Certificates) Regulations 1993 (SI 1993/125) and the European Communities (Legal Protection of Biotechnological Inventions) Regulations 2000 (SI 2000/247).

Under the 1964 Act, patents were granted with a term of 16 years. There was provision for an extension of that term. If the court or Controller, as the case may have been, having regard to the nature and merits of the invention in relation to the public and to the profits made by the patentee as such and all the circumstances of the case, found that the patentee had been inadequately remunerated by his patent, then the term of the patent could be extended for a further period not exceeding five years or, in exceptional cases, 10 years. The 1963 Act served its purpose well, but in view of Ireland's membership of the then European Community and other international conventions it became necessary to replace the 1963 Act in its entirety.

Patents granted under PA92 are for a term of 20 years. However, there is a provision for the grant of short term patents which have a term of 10 years.

Under the transitional provisions of PA92 the term of any patent granted under the 1964 Act and which was in force at the commencement of PA92 was extended to 20 years. However, during the final two years of the term of such a patent, it is not an infringement to make preparations for putting the invention into effect after the patent expires, provided that this does not include importation or marketing of the patented product.

Some provisions of the 1964 Act may still be relevant, eg a patent granted under the 1964 Act is revocable only in accordance with the provisions of the 1964 Act. All patents granted from 1 August 1992 onwards have been granted under the 1992 Act.

4.2 International conventions

4.2.1 Paris Convention for the Protection of Industrial Property, 1883–1967

The International Convention for the Protection of Industrial Property (signed in Paris in 1883) provides that, as regards the protection of industrial property, each member country shall afford to nationals of other member countries the same protection as it affords to its own nationals and that the filing of an application for a patent in one member country gives a right of priority to the date of that application in respect of corresponding applications filed in other member countries within 12 months of that date. Ireland formally acceded to the Paris Convention in 1925.

4.2.2   Patent Co-operation Treaty 1970

The Patent Co-operation Treaty (PCT) created an international system for lodging applications for the grant of patents. The applications are subjected to an International Search and (at the option of the applicant) an International Preliminary Examination. The applications are then sent to national or regional patent offices for completion of the grant procedure. Ireland joined the PCT in 1992.

4.2.3   European Patent Convention 1973

The European Patent Convention (EPC) established a common system of law for the grant of patents in European countries (including some non-EC members), and led to the opening of the European Patent Office (EPO) in Munich and The Hague in 1977. An application to the EPO leads to the grant of a single European patent, but this takes effect as a bundle of national patents, in selected states designated by the applicant. Ireland joined the EPC in 1992, and the law on patentability in PA92 is derived from it.

4.2.4   Agreement relating to Community Patents incorporating the Community Patent Convention (CPC) 1975–89

This Agreement was an attempt by the then EC countries to provide that the European patent granted by the EPO would have unitary effect in the Community. It has never entered into force but it is the source of the national law applied to granted patents in EU Member States, including Ireland.

4.3   Patentability

4.3.1   Patentable inventions

Section 9(1) of PA92 provides that an invention shall be patentable if it is susceptible of industrial application, is new and involves an inventive step. An invention is considered as susceptible of industrial application if it can be made or used in any kind of industry, including agriculture (s 14 of PA92).
    Section 9(2) provides that any of the following shall not be regarded as an invention within the meaning of s 9(1):

(a) a discovery, a scientific theory or a mathematical method;
(b) an aesthetic creation;
(c) a scheme, rule or method for performing a mental act, playing a game or doing business, or a program for a computer;
(d) the presentation of information.

Section 9(3) provides that the provisions of s 9(2) shall exclude patentability of subject matter or activities referred to in that subsection only to the extent to which a patent application or patent relates to such subject matter or activities as such.

Section 9(4) provides that a method for treatment of the human or animal body by surgery or therapy and a diagnostic method practised on the human or animal body shall not be regarded as an invention susceptible of industrial application for the purposes of s 9(1). The proviso to the subsection provides that the provisions of the subsection shall not apply to a product, and in particular a substance or composition, for use in any such method. Pharmaceutical compositions are, of course, the subject of many valuable patents. It is worth noting that although methods of medical treatment are excluded from patenting in Ireland (and other EPC countries), they can be patented in the US.

Section 9(5) gives power to the Minister by order to modify any of the provisions of ss 9, 10 (other than para (a)) and 11 for the purpose of giving effect, in relation to the patentability of inventions, to the EPC as amended by any international treaty, convention or agreement to which the State is or proposes to become a party.

It will be seen, therefore, that there are four basic requirements for patentability:

(a) there must be an 'invention';
(b) the invention must be 'susceptible of industrial application';
(c) the invention must be 'new';
(d) the invention must include 'an inventive step'.

There is no definition of 'invention' in PA92 but s 9(2) contains a non-exhaustive list of things which are not to be regarded as inventions. Likewise there is no definition of 'invention' in the EPC but Rule 27 of the Rules made under the EPC says the following:

> The description shall:
>
> (a) specify the technical field to which the invention relates;
> (b) ...
> (c) disclose the invention ... in such terms that the technical problem ... and its solution can be understood ...

These references to 'technical field' and 'technical problem' are taken as authority for requiring that an invention should have a technical character.

Some examples of patentable inventions include:

(a) machines and mechanical devices;
(b) electronic and telecommunications equipment;
(c) computer hardware and systems;
(d) computer-implemented inventions;
(e) pharmaceuticals and agrochemicals;
(f) biotech products and methods;
(g) manufacturing processes;
(h) methods for treating materials;
(i) improvements in any of the above.

It will be noted that under s 9(3) a computer program is excluded from patentability 'only to the extent to which a patent or patent application relates to such subject matter ... as such'. The equivalent exclusion in the EPC is narrowly interpreted in the EPO. If the subject matter of an invention makes a technical contribution to the known art, patentability will not be denied merely on the ground that a computer program is included in its implementation. Program-controlled machines and program-controlled manufacturing and control processes should normally be regarded as patentable subject matter. Various ways of claiming protection for computer-implemented inventions are available, and it should not be assumed that computer software or business systems cannot be patented. The law has been under extensive discussion in Europe, both before and after the circulation of a draft EU directive on the patentability of computer-implemented inventions, COM (2002) 92 final; 2002/0047 (COD). Also, the law in the US is different from that in Europe and permits patent claims to software and business methods. Even if a patent can only be obtained in the US, this may well be the most valuable market for the inventor. Meanwhile, the basic protection in Europe for computer programs *per se* is under copyright law.

4.3.2 Novelty and inventive step

Novelty and inventive step are different criteria. Novelty exists if there is any difference between the invention and the known art. There must first be novelty before there can be an inventive step.

Section 11(1) of PA92 provides that an invention shall be considered to be new if it does not form part of the state of the art. Section 11(2) provides that the state of the art shall be held to comprise everything made available to the public (whether in the State or elsewhere) by means of a written or oral description, by use, or in any other way, before the date of filing of the patent application. Where the invention is disclosed to the public before the date of filing of the patent application then the invention is said to be anticipated and a patent, even if granted, is likely to be invalid. 'The public' includes any person or organisation not in a relationship of confidentiality with the inventor(s) or their employers. It is crucially important, therefore, that a patent application is filed before any publication of the invention. In practice, this can cause particular problems for inventions arising from university research, where the pressure for early publication has to be balanced against the wish to obtain patent protection. Even an oral contribution at a conference can amount to disclosure.

Section 11(3) provides that in addition, the content of a patent application as filed, of which the date of filing is prior to the date of filing the Irish application and which was published under PA92 (or, by virtue of the transitional provisions, the 1964 Act) on or after that date, shall be considered as comprised in the state of the art. Thus, the novelty of a later application has to be judged against the content of an earlier unpublished application. However, the earlier application is not considered in deciding whether or not there has been an inventive step (s 13 of PA92).

Section 11(4) provides that the provisions of s 11(1), (2) and (3) shall not exclude the patentability of any substance or composition, comprised in the state of the art, for use in a method for the treatment of the human or animal body provided that its use for such method is not already comprised in the state of the art. Therefore a substance that is already known for a non-medical use can be patented when it is first found to be useful in a method of medical treatment.

An inventor faces the risk of anticipation on two fronts, first from independent inventors and secondly from those persons whose information comes from the same source as his own. In the latter case, a disloyal employee can disclose the invention to a third party, or a third party to whom the invention was disclosed in confidence can breach that confidence. In the absence of any statutory provisions, those disclosures would prejudice an application for a patent on the basis that the relevant invention was anticipated. Section 12 was enacted to give limited relief in such circumstances. The section relates to disclosures which are non-prejudicial. The section provides that disclosures which occur not earlier than six months preceding the filing of the patent application do not form part of the state of the art if disclosure was due, or in consequence of, a breach of confidence or agreement in relation to, or the unlawful obtaining of the matter constituting the invention. The same applies if the applicant has displayed the invention at certain specified international exhibitions.

4.3.3 Short term patents (Pt III of PA92, ss 63–67)

Short term patents are granted for a term of 10 years. An invention is patentable as a short term patent if it is new and susceptible of industrial application, provided it is not clearly lacking an inventive step. This definition is intended to set a somewhat lower threshold of inventiveness for a short term patent. No novelty search is required before a short term patent is granted.

It is not possible to have a short term patent and a full term patent for the same invention. Where an application for a short term patent and a full term patent are filed by the same applicant in respect of the same invention then the short term patent, if granted first, shall be deemed void upon the grant of the full term patent, or in the event that the application for the short term patent is pending at the date of grant of the full term patent then the application is deemed to be abandoned at that date.

A drawback of a short term patent is that infringement proceedings may not be commenced without going through the procedure laid down in s 66. Section 66(1) provides that the proprietor must first request the Controller to cause a search to be undertaken in relation to the invention and a report of the results of the search to be prepared and furnish a copy to the proposed defendant.

There is an alternative procedure under s 66(3) under which it is possible to submit the results of a search carried out in a prescribed foreign state (the UK or Germany), or under a convention (the EPC) or treaty (the PCT) in respect of the same invention.

Proceedings for infringement of a short term patent may be brought in the circuit court irrespective of the value of a claim.

There is an additional ground for revocation of a short term patent, namely, that the claims of the specification of the patent are not supported by the description.

4.3.4 Supplementary Protection Certificates

On 2 January 1992, Council Regulation EEC/1768/92 concerning the creation of Supplementary Protection Certificates (SPCs) for medicinal products was published. It was given effect in Ireland by SI 1993/125. The SPC recognises that the period of time between filing a patent application and obtaining regulatory approval to market a new medicinal product can mean that the effective period of patent protection is very much reduced. This placed European industry at a disadvantage when compared with other jurisdictions where patent term restoration provisions had been introduced.

A similar system of SPCs for plant protection products was introduced by Council Regulation EC/1610/96. No statutory instrument was required to bring it into effect in Ireland as SI 1993/125 was considered to be sufficient.

Once an SPC has been granted it will not take effect until the end of the term of the basic patent. It confers the same rights as the patent but only in respect of the medicinal or plant protection product for which a marketing authorisation was issued. The maximum life of any SPC in Ireland is five years. The period of protection is equal to the period which elapsed between the date of the filing of the application for the basic patent and the date of the first marketing authorisation in the EU reduced by a period of five years. In any event, the duration of the SPC in Ireland is not to exceed five years.

4.4 Ideas and know-how

Ideas are generally not patentable unless they have some potential industrial application. As already noted, s 9(2) of PA92 excludes such items as a discovery, a scientific theory, or a scheme for performing a mental act from being regarded as an invention. Know-how has been defined by Commission Regulation EC/240/96 as:

> A body of technical information that is secret, substantial and identified in any appropriate form.

It usually consists of industrial information or techniques likely to assist in the manufacture or processing of goods or materials, and of potential value to a competitor or licensee. Know-how may include something patentable but it often lacks an inventive step.

4.4.1 Patent v know-how

In deciding whether to apply for a patent or to retain secret know-how, various advantages and disadvantages must be balanced:

(a) Advantages of a patent:
- exclusive statutory right for up to 20 years;
- scope of protection defined;
- no need for secrecy after a full patent application has been made.

(b) Disadvantages of a patent:
- the invention is published after 18 months from the date of the first patent application;
- after the invention has been published, a patent may be refused or revoked because of lack of novelty or inventive step.

(c) Advantages of know-how:
- with good controls on confidential information, know-how may be kept secret for the whole working life of a product or process.

(d) Disadvantages of know-how:
- not protected if it gets into the public domain or if someone else devises it independently;
- lack of clarity as to what is protected;
- competitor may deduce it by analysing the product.

4.5 Applying for a patent

If a solicitor is consulted by a client about a new invention, it is usual to refer the client to a patent agent for advice and, if appropriate, for preparation of a patent application.

4.5.1 Novelty searches

As a first step, a patent agent will usually recommend that a search should be carried out to check whether the invention appears to be new. Database searches can be done among previous patents, or in abstracts or full texts of technical literature. Searches can also be performed in classified paper collections of patents. Most relevant prior art is often found in the inventor's own literature collection. However, it is not obligatory to carry out a preliminary search. A decision may be made to wait for an official search report from a patent office after an application has been filed (eg, under s 29 of PA92).

4.5.2 Preparing a patent application (ss 18–22 of PA92)

A patent agent drafts a specification, which should contain the elements set out in s 18(2) of PA92:

(a) A description of the invention, accompanied by drawings if appropriate to the type of invention concerned. The description must disclose the invention in a manner sufficiently clear and complete for it to be carried out by another person skilled in the technical field (s 19 of PA92).

(b) One or more claims, placed after the description. The claim or claims define the matter for which patent protection is sought. They should also be clear and concise and be supported by the description (s 20 of PA92). In practice the patent agent will draft a set of claims, starting with the broadest scope that can be justified by the novel contribution made by the invention, as compared to the prior art. Several aspects of the invention or a group of inventions (eg, a product, process, apparatus, etc) may be claimed in one application, provided that they are so linked as to form a single inventive concept (s 21 of PA92).

(c) An abstract, which serves for use as technical information, eg for entry into databases for searching purposes. It is not to be used for interpreting the scope of patent protection sought.

4.5.3 Filing a first Irish patent application (s 18(1), (3); s 63(5) of PA92)

The Irish Patents Office is based in Kilkenny but also retains a filing office in Dublin. The initial application may be made for either:

(a) a short term patent for 10 years (a short term patent can be granted quickly because there is no requirement for a search or evidence of novelty of the invention before grant); or

(b) a full term patent for 20 years. In the case of a full term patent, the applicant must either request an official search (s 29 of PA92) or submit evidence of search results or of the grant of a patent for the same invention in a prescribed foreign state (Great Britain or Germany), or under a convention (the EPC) or treaty (the PCT). The applicant must then amend the application in the light of the evidence relied upon (usually called the 'evidence of novelty') or must file a statement that no amendment is considered necessary (s 30 of PA92). When submitting such an amendment or statement, the applicant must be represented by a patent agent (Rule 93(2) of PR92).

4.5.4 Filing a first application elsewhere

Instead of starting with an application for an Irish patent, the applicant may decide to file a European application initially in order to get the results of a full EPO search at an early date. Alternatively, because of differences between European and US law, it may in some cases be sensible to send the first application to the US Patent and Trade Mark Office.

4.5.5 Claiming priority (ss 25–27 of PA92 and Art 4 of the Paris Convention)

During a period of 12 months after filing the first application, the applicant (or a successor in title) may make a subsequent application to patent the same invention and can effectively get the subsequent application back-dated to the first filing date, thus enjoying a right of priority over a later applicant. This can be done both in Ireland and in any country or region abroad which belongs to the Paris Convention (s 25 of PA92). The 12-month period should allow the inventor or other owner of the invention to investigate its commercial potential before incurring the expense of an international patent filing programme, although in practice the time runs out very quickly.

4.5.6 Patenting an invention in Europe (European Patent Convention; ss 118–24 of PA92)

It is possible to apply for national patents in individual European countries but translation of the text is generally required at the outset (except of course in the UK). Instead, an application at the EPO can designate up to 24 States and can be presented in English. The application is subjected to official search and examination at the EPO. If and when it proceeds to grant, the European Patent takes effect as a bundle of patents in the designated states. Under current arrangements, a translation is then required in most states, but the applicant can decide to abandon protection in a number of countries if the translation costs are too high.

Since Ireland joined the EPC in 1992, the majority of applicants from other countries have used the EPO route to obtain patent protection here. A European patent designating the State is treated from its date of grant as a patent granted under the 1992 Act (s 119 of PA92). If the European patent is not published in English (ie, is in French or German), an English translation must be filed at the Irish Patents Office within six months from the date of grant (s 119(6) of PA92 and Rule 83 of PR92).

A European patent can be opposed at the EPO by a third party during nine months after grant. If the patent is amended or revoked as a result of the opposition, the amendment or revocation has automatic effect in Ireland (s 119(4) of PA92).

4.5.7 Applying internationally (Patent Co-operation Treaty; s 127 of PA92)

As in Europe, it is possible to apply for national patents in countries in other parts of the world, such as the US, Canada, Japan, Australia, etc. However, an application under the PCT can designate up to 115 States as well as regional patent offices including the EPO. The PCT application is subjected to an international search and (at the applicant's option) to an International Preliminary Examination. Then, usually after two and a half years from the priority date, the application goes forward into national processing in individual countries and/or regional processing at the EPO and other regional offices, where patents are granted or refused. The PCT provides an international system for filing applications but does not establish an international patent.

4.6 Ownership of the right to a patent (ss 15–16, 79–80 of PA92)

Section 15 provides that any person may make an application for a patent either alone or jointly with another. Section 16 then provides that the right to a patent belongs to the inventor or his successor in title, but if the inventor is an employee the right to a patent shall be determined in accordance with the law of the State in which the employee is wholly or mainly employed or, if the identity of such state cannot be determined, in accordance with the law of the State in which the employer has his place of business to which the employee is attached. Section 16(2) goes on to provide that if two or more persons have made an invention independently of each other, the right to a patent for the invention shall belong to the person whose patent application has the earliest or earlier (as the case may be appropriate) date of filing, but the provisions shall only apply if the earliest or earlier application has been duly published under PA92.

In Ireland ownership of employee inventions is determined by common law, which provides that an invention made by an employee belongs to an employer:

(a) if the invention is made in the course of the normal duties of the employee or in the course of duties falling outside his normal duties, but specifically assigned to him, and if the circumstances in either case were such that an invention might reasonably be expected to result from the carrying out of his duties; or

(b) the invention was made in the course of the duties of the employee and, at the time of making the invention, because of the nature of his duties and the particular responsibilities arising from the nature of his duties, he had a special obligation to further the interests of the employer's undertaking.

Unlike the UK, there is no statutory provision in Ireland which provides for compensation to employees in respect of inventions made in the course of employment.

4.6.1 Co-ownership of patent applications and patents (s 80 of PA92)

This section deals with co-ownership. Section 80(1) provides that where a patent is applied for by, or is granted to, two or more persons, each of those persons shall, unless an agreement to the contrary is in force, be entitled to an equal undivided share in common in the patent application or patent, as the case may be.

Section 80(2) provides that subject to the provisions of the section where two or more persons are entered in the register as applicants for or proprietors of a patent, then, unless an agreement to the contrary is in force, each of those persons shall be entitled, by himself or his agents, to do in respect of the invention concerned for his own benefit without accounting to the others any act which would, apart from the subsection, amount to an infringement of the patent application or patent concerned.

Section 80(6) provides that nothing in s 80(1) or s 80(2) shall affect the mutual rights or obligations of trustees or of the personal representatives of a deceased person, or their rights or obligations as such. Accordingly the undivided share of a co-owner of a patent or an application devolves upon his personal representatives.

Section 80(3), (4) and (5) cover certain dealings by a co-owner of a patent or patent application. Section 80(3) provides that a co-owner may not grant a licence or assign his share without the consent of all the other co-owners. As mentioned in 4.7.2 below, a patent can be indirectly infringed by a third party, not having the patent owner's consent, applying or offering to supply in the State a party, other than a party entitled to exploit a patented invention, with the means, relating to an essential element of that invention, for putting it into effect, when the third party knows, or it is obvious in the circumstances to a reasonable person, that the said means are suitable and intended for putting that invention into effect. Section 80(4) allows a third party to supply a co-owner with means, relating to an essential element of the relevant invention, for putting the invention into effect without being guilty of indirect infringement. Section 80(5) provides that where a co-owner sells a product covered by the co-owned invention, then the purchaser and any person claiming through him is entitled to deal with it in the same manner as if the product had been sold by a sole owner.

Section 79 of PA92 provides that subject to s 80 (which deals with co-ownership of patent applications and patents) the rules of law applicable to the ownership and devolution of personal property shall apply in relation to patent applications and patents as they apply in relation to other choses in action.

4.7 Infringement (ss 40–46 of PA92)

Before considering whether there has been infringement, it is first necessary to construe the claims of a patent. If the relevant product or process does not fall within the claims, properly construed, then there can be no infringement. The relevant date for construction of the patent is the date of publication of the specification.

The 1992 Act has statutory provisions relating to construction. Section 45(1) provides that the extent of the protection conferred by a patent shall be determined by the terms of the claims; nevertheless, the description and drawing shall be used to interpret the claims. Section 45(3) provides that the court shall have regard to the directions contained in the Protocol on the Interpretation of Art 69 of the European Patent Convention and set out in Sched 2 to the Act. This endeavours to define a compromise position between strict and liberal interpretation 'which combines a fair protection for the patentee with a reasonable degree of certainty for third parties'. For an illustration of the construction of patent claims under the same Protocol in England, see the Court of Appeal judgments in *Wheatley (Davina) v Drillsafe Ltd* [2001] RPC 133.

Knowledge on the part of the infringer of the invention or patent is normally irrelevant. Whether or not the infringer intended to infringe is also irrelevant. It is not necessary for the patentee to suffer damage in order for there to be infringement.

The onus is on the plaintiff to prove infringement. He must provide sufficient evidence to establish infringement on the balance of probabilities. There is a statutory exception to this rule. Section 46 provides that if the subject matter of a patent is a process for obtaining a new product, the same product when produced by a person other than the proprietor or applicant, as the case may be, shall, in the absence of sufficient evidence to raise an issue as to whether the product was obtained by that or another process, be deemed to have been obtained by the process which is such subject matter.

Section 40 makes it clear that infringement only occurs if a person does specified things 'in the State' without the proprietor's consent. Section 117 declares that the Act applies to the waters in the portion of the sea which comprises the territorial seas of the State, the waters in all the areas of the sea to which the internal or inland waters of the State are extended by s 5 of the Maritime Jurisdiction Act 1959, and the waters in any area which is for the time being a designated area within the meaning of s 1 of the Continental Shelf Act 1968.

4.7.1 Direct infringing acts (s 40 of PA92)

A patent, while it is in force, confers on its proprietor the right to prevent all third parties not having his consent from doing in the State all or any of the following things:

(a) making, offering, putting on the market or using a product which is the subject matter of the patent, or importing or stocking the product for those purposes;

(b) using a process which is the subject matter of the patent;

(c) offering, putting on the market, using or importing, or stocking for those purposes, the product obtained directly by a process which is the subject matter of the patent.

It will be noted that the classic infringing acts are included, ie making a patented product and using a patented process. After manufacture, the list of infringing acts covers offering, putting on the market, using or importing or stocking a patented product or a product obtained directly by a patented process. Where patented goods pass down the distribution chain each person in that chain becomes an infringer in his capacity as offeror and putting the infringing product on the market. The ultimate recipient will be an infringer if he is a user.

4.7.2   Indirect infringement

Prior to the enactment of PA92, the courts were reluctant to treat as a contributory infringer someone who assisted in preparations for infringing acts within the claims but did not himself perform those infringing acts. Only where the person who assisted in the preparations actually ordered the other party to infringe, or participated in a conspiracy or common design to secure performance or knowingly induced another person to perform, would any liability in tort be imposed.

Although the marginal note to s 40 refers to prevention of direct use of an invention, s 40(b) does cover a form of indirect infringement. It is an infringement to offer a process for use in the State knowing that the user will have no licence from the proprietor of the patent and that the use will be an infringement. Both the offer and use must be in the State and the knowledge of the person who offers the process is judged objectively, taking account of what is obvious to a reasonable person in the circumstances.

Section 41(1) provides that a patent while it is in force shall also confer on its proprietor the right to prevent all third parties not having his consent from supplying or offering to supply in the state a person, other than a party entitled to exploit the patented invention, with the means, relating to an essential element of that invention, for putting it into effect therein, when the third party knows, or it is obvious in the circumstances to a reasonable person, that the said means are suitable and intended for putting that invention into effect.

This subsection would cover the situation where the third party supplies a product in kit form to be assembled into an infringing article by the purchaser.

Section 41(2) provides that s 41(1) shall not apply when the means referred to therein are staple commercial products, except when the third party induces the person supplied to commit acts which the proprietor of a patent is enabled to prevent by virtue of s 40.

There is no definition of staple commercial products. It is assumed that the word staple is a reference to raw materials or other basic products commonly available. The purpose of the subsection is to protect the supplier of such products even if he has knowledge that they are to be put to an infringing purpose.

Section 44(3) provides that persons performing acts referred to in s 42(a), (b) or (c) shall not be considered to be parties entitled to exploit an invention pursuant to s 41(1).

The person or persons who actually perform the infringing act are liable to the patentee. A person can infringe a patent by making the article himself, or by his agent, or by his servant. The agent and servants themselves can infringe the patent, and actions can be brought against them individually but that does not absolve the person who employed them for that purpose.

Persons may be liable for infringement if their acts are such as would make them joint tortfeasors under the general law. Before a person can be said to be a joint tortfeasor, he must have acted in concert with another person in the commission of the tort.

4.8   Action for infringement

Section 85(7) of PA92 provides the sanction for non-registration of registerable documents, eg an assignment of a patent and an exclusive licence. A document in respect of which no entry has been made in the register under s 85(3) shall only be admitted in any court as evidence of title of any person to a patent application or share of or interest in a patent application or patent if the court so directs. Similarly, the holder of an exclusive licence may also be delayed in instituting an action under s 51.

Section 51(1) provides that an exclusive licensee has the like right as the patentee to take proceedings in respect of any infringement of the patent committed after the date of the licence, and in awarding damages or granting any other relief in the proceedings the court shall take into consideration any loss suffered or likely to be suffered by the exclusive licensee as a result of the infringement or, as the case may be, the profits derived from the infringement, so far as it constitutes an infringement of the rights of the exclusive licensee as such.

Section 51(2) provides that in proceedings taken by an exclusive licensee, unless the patentee is joined as plaintiff in the proceedings, he must be added as a defendant, provided that a patentee added as a defendant in pursuance of the subsection is not liable for any costs unless he enters an appearance and takes part in the proceedings. A sole licensee has no right to take an infringement action.

Section 95 gives power to the High Court in an action or proceeding for infringement or revocation of a patent to call in aid an assessor specially qualified in the opinion of the court and try the case wholly or partially with his assistance.

Section 95(2) gives a similar power to the Supreme Court.

4.9 Remedies for infringement

Remedies for infringement are as follows:

(a) injunction;
(b) damages and account of profits;
(c) order for delivery up or destruction;
(d) relief for infringement of partially valid patent;
(e) certificate of contested validity;
(f) costs.

Under the terms of s 47 of PA92, in infringement proceedings a claim may be made for:

(a) an injunction restraining the defendant from infringing;
(b) an order requiring the defendant to deliver up or destroy any product covered by the patent;
(c) damages;
(d) an account of profits derived by the defendant from the alleged infringement;
(e) a declaration that the patent is valid and has been infringed by the defendant.

Section 47(2) provides that the court shall not, in respect of the same infringement, both award the patentee damages and order that the plaintiff shall be given an account of the profits.

The grant of an injunction is a discretionary matter, and the court retains a discretion to refuse an injunction and award damages in lieu. However, the court will only refuse an injunction in an exceptional case.

The ordinary form of injunction is:

> ... that the defendants, by themselves, their servants or agents be restrained from infringing patent No [...].

Until recently, in the UK, an injunction not to infringe a patent could not be effective after the patent had ceased to be in force. A post-patent injunction was granted in the case of *Dyson Appliances Ltd v Hoover Ltd* [2001] RPC 544. The injunction, granted to Dyson, was to restrain manufacture and sale of certain Hoover vacuum cleaners after the expiration date of a Dyson patent that would have infringed the patent when it was in force. This followed a finding in October 2000 that Hoover had infringed a patent in relation to groundbreaking technology. Until the decision, 'post-expiry' injunctions were seen to be at odds with the limited 20-year monopoly granted under the patent system. Dyson asked the court to prevent Hoover from manufacturing and selling any vacuum cleaners which would have infringed the Dyson patent (or alternatively to prevent them from recommencing sales of their Vortex vacuum cleaner which had been held to infringe) for a period of 12 months after expiry of the patent.

The judge ruled that in the absence of a post-expiry injunction Hoover would be able to recommence selling its Vortex cleaner soon after expiry of the patent, as it had 'jumped the gun', having already carried out all the necessary development work and obtained a requisite product authorisation. Hoover's re-entry into the UK market would be boosted by the fact that the product had already been sold for about 18 months before Dyson secured its judgment. The judge felt that Hoover should not be able to gain a 'springboard' by which it could compete with Dyson almost as soon as the patent expired. Furthermore, an accurate assessment of damages would be 'notoriously difficult' and therefore, 'prevention was better than cure'.

4.9.1 Damages and account of profits

A successful patentee is entitled to damages in respect of actual infringement of his patent or, at his option, an account of profits. The patentee is entitled to disclosure from the defendant to enable him to choose between damages or profits.

4.9.1.1 Restriction on recovery of damages for infringement (s 49 of PA92)

The courts have always been reluctant to award damages against a person who innocently infringes a common law right, but they have always been willing to grant injunctions to prevent continued infringement. Section 49(1) provides that in proceedings for infringement of a patent damages shall not be awarded, and no order shall be made for an account of profits against a defendant who proves that at the date of the infringement he was not aware, and had no reasonable grounds for supposing, that that patent existed, and a person shall not be deemed to have been so aware or to have had reasonable grounds for so supposing by reason only of the application to a product of the word 'patent' or 'patented' or any word or words expressing or implying that a patent has been obtained for the product, unless the number of the relevant patent accompanied the word or words in question. The requirement of reasonableness means that a defendant who copies a new product ought to enquire whether it is patented. The proviso to the subsection suggests that the courts will take a reasonable approach.

Section 49(2) provides that in proceedings for infringement of a patent the court may, if it thinks fit, refuse to award any damages or make any order in respect of any infringement committed during an extension period specified in a late request for renewal under s 36(3) but before the payment of the renewal fee and any additional fee prescribed for the purpose of that subsection.

Section 36(3) provides that where an amendment of a specification of a patent has been allowed under the Act, no damages shall be awarded in any proceedings for an infringement of the patent committed before the date of the decision allowing the amendment, unless the court is satisfied that the specification of the patent, as originally published, was framed in good faith and with reasonable skill and knowledge. The principle to be applied when assessing damages is that the plaintiff should be restored by monetary compensation to the position which he would have occupied but for the wrongful acts of the defendant, provided always that such loss as he proves is the natural and direct consequence of the defendant's act.

Section 51 provides that in awarding damages or granting any other relief to an exclusive licensee who sues as plaintiff, the court must take into consideration only the loss suffered or likely to be suffered by the actual exclusive licensee. If the exclusive licensee claims an account of profits in lieu of damages, the profits to be considered are those earned by means of the infringement so far as it constitutes an infringement of the rights of the exclusive licensee as such.

4.9.2 Delivery up or destruction

Section 47(1)(a) of PA92 gives power to the court to order that the infringing goods be delivered up to the patent owner or that they be destroyed. This is to ensure that the infringing goods are not retained in order to be placed on the market after the expiry of the patent. If such an order were not available then the infringer could profit after patent expiry from the sale of goods that were manufactured at the time the patent was in force.

4.9.3 Relief for infringement of partially valid patent

By s 50 of PA92, where in infringement proceedings a patent has been found to be only partially valid, relief may be granted in respect of that part of it which has been found to be valid and infringed; provided that the court shall not grant relief by way of damages or costs except in circumstances that are mentioned in s 50(2). Section 50(2) provides that where in proceedings for the infringement of a patent the plaintiff proves that the specification of the patent was framed in good faith and with reasonable skill and knowledge, the court may grant relief in respect of that part of the patent which is valid and infringed, subject to the discretion of the court as to costs and as to the date from which damages should be reckoned.

4.9.4 Certificate of contested validity

Section 52 provides that if in any proceedings before the court the validity of a patent to any extent is contested and the patent is found by the court to be wholly or partially valid, the court may certify the finding and the fact that validity of the patent was contested. Section 52(2) provides that where such a certificate has been granted then if in any subsequent proceedings before the court for infringement of the patent or before the court or the Controller for revocation of the patent, a final order or judgment is made or given in favour of the party relying on the validity of the patent, that party shall, unless the court otherwise directs, be entitled to his costs as between solicitor and own client. The purpose of this provision is in order to prevent a patentee from being put repeatedly to the expense of defending successive attacks on the validity of his patent.

4.9.5 Costs

In the usual way, a successful patentee in an infringement action would be entitled to his costs. As in any other court proceedings, costs are discretionary but usually follow the event.

4.10 Defences and statutory exceptions to infringement

4.10.1 Consent of the proprietor of the patent

It is a prerequisite of infringement under s 40 that the act complained of should be done without the consent of the proprietor of the patent. There is no requirement that this consent should be express and the normal rules of law will apply to determine whether consent is to be implied.

4.10.2 Euro-defences

Limitation of rights is dealt with under s 43 of PA92. The rights conferred by a patent shall not extend to any act which, pursuant to any obligations imposed by the law of the Treaty of Rome Establishing the European Communities, cannot be prevented by the proprietor of the patent.

Acts which cannot be prevented fall into three broad areas: Arts 28–30 of the Treaty (formerly Art 30, 34 and Art 36), Art 81(1) (formerly Art 85(1)) and Art 82 (formerly Art 86).

A person who relies on the provisions of these Articles in defence to an infringement action is said to be relying on 'Euro-defences'.

In order to succeed in a Euro-defence, the defendant must establish a connection between the attempted enforcement of the patent rights and the alleged infringement of the Treaty:

> The nexus required is ... that the exercise of the exclusive right as sought by the plaintiff in the pleadings would involve a breach of the Treaty (*Ransburg-Gema AJ v Electrostatic Plant Systems Ltd* [1991] FSR 508, CA, *per* Aldous J).

> It is sufficient that the existence of the intellectual property right creates or buttresses the dominant position which the plaintiff is abusing. The remedy contemplated by the court [in *Volvo v Veng*] is that the plaintiff may have to be deprived of the means of maintaining his dominant position *(Pitney Bowes Inc v Francotyp-Postalia GmbH* [1991] FSR 72, Ch D, *per* Hoffmann J).

Patent rights raise particular difficulty under EU competition law. The EU has endeavoured to balance the rights of the patent owner which are monopolistic with free competition in a single market. A patent owner has, for a period of years, the right to use his invention or to sell the products covered by his patent. He has the right to dispose of the patent entirely or to license others to use the invention for the whole of the territory where the patent rights exist or a defined part of that territory. The existence of such rights and the terms upon which licences are granted may restrict competition.

The purpose of the EU single market is to establish a single market among all EU Member States, ie one national market throughout the European Union. If intellectual property rights applied throughout the Union there would be no great difficulty in achieving this. Apart from the community trade mark, which, when granted by the Community Trade Mark Office in Alicante covers the entire Union, intellectual property rights are essentially national. Therefore, as a matter of law a patent owner in one Member State may, in certain circumstances, prevent the importation of products covered by his patent lawfully marketed in another Member State by suing for infringement of his patent and thereby obstruct the free movement of goods.

In resolving the conflict between national patent rights and free movement of goods, the ECJ has relied on the principles under Arts 28–30 (formerly Arts 30, 34 and 36). Article 28 prohibits all quantitative restrictions and measures having equivalent effect on imports and exports between Member States. The right of the owner of a national patent to bring an action against an importer *prima facie* constitutes a measure having equivalent effect. The right given by the Patents Act 1992 to the owner of a patent to bring an infringement action must therefore be justified under Art 30 which provides that the prohibition in Art 28 is subject to an exception if the measure in question is 'justified on grounds of ... the protection of industrial and commercial property'. In determining the extent of the protection offered by Art 30, the ECJ has drawn a distinction between the 'existence' and the 'exercise' of intellectual property rights and held that it is only the 'existence' of the right which is protected by Art 30 and that the 'exercise' of the right is subject to limitations arising from the rules of the Treaty.

The ECJ has also developed another important principle known as 'exhaustion of rights'. The ECJ has held that Arts 28–30 provide a complete defence to an infringement action if it is shown that the products in question have been previously marketed in another Member State by the proprietor of that right or with his consent. The previous marketing is said to have 'exhausted' the ability of the owner of the right to prevent the subsequent free circulation of the products concerned throughout the Union.

Under Arts 28–30, the effect of the rules on free movement of goods on actions for patent infringement may be summarised as follows:

(a) Arts 28–30 of the Treaty preclude the proprietor of a patent protected by the law of one Member State from suing for infringement to prevent the importation of a product that has been lawfully marketed in another Member State by the proprietor or with his consent. This is the 'exhaustion of rights' principle and applies even if the product is not patentable in the latter Member State.

(b) The effect of Arts 28–30 is not finally decided in the case of a direct sale into one Member State by a patent licensee or assignee in another Member State where the goods in question have not been previously marketed in the latter Member State.

(c) Arts 28–30 of the Treaty do not preclude the exercise of patent rights to prevent the importation into the European Union of goods originating in third countries.

(d) Arts 28–30 do not otherwise affect actions for infringement, unless it is shown that for some other reason the infringement action is not 'justified for the protection of industrial or commercial property rights', or amounts to 'arbitrary discrimination' or a 'disguised restriction on trade between Member States' within the meaning of the second sentence of Art 36.

Under Art 81(1) (formerly Art 85(1)), although intellectual property rights do not as such fall within Art 81(1), the bringing of an infringement action may contravene Art 81(1) where the infringement action tends to the partitioning of the common market and is brought as 'the object, the means or the consequence' of an agreement.

Under Art 82 (formerly Art 86), according to the recent case law of the Courts of Justice and of First Instance, the improper exercise of an intellectual property right is capable of infringing Art 82. However, for Art 82 to apply it is necessary to establish:

(a) a dominant position in a relevant product and geographic market in a substantial part of the common market; and

(b) an abuse of that position in a manner likely to affect trade between Member States.

When considering how best to defend a patent infringement action, consideration should always be given as to whether it is possible to plead one or more of the Euro-defences. When the defendant is importing the patentee's own product from another EU Member State consideration should first be given to whether the parallel import 'defence' is available. Consideration should then be given as to whether there are any agreements relating to the patent in suit which may be contrary to Art 81(1). Finally, consideration should be given to whether an Art 82 defence is available. In order to successfully plead such a defence the defendant will need to establish dominance in a relevant market, abusive conduct, a connection between the alleged abuse and the infringement action and connection between the abuse and an effect on trade between Member States. None of these matters are easy or cheap to prove.

4.10.3 Infringement not novel

No relief could be obtained in respect of an invalid patent. If the defendant can prove that the act complained of was merely what was disclosed in a publication which could be relied on against the validity of the patent, without any substantial or patentable variation having been made, he has a good defence. This is the so-called 'Gillette defence'.

4.10.4 Patent invalid

More generally, the validity of a patent may be put in issue by way of a counterclaim in infringement proceedings. The grounds of invalidity must be one of the grounds specified in s 58 of PA92 on which the patent could be revoked (see below).

4.10.5 Right to continue use begun before priority date

Under s 55, where a patent is granted for an invention, a person who in the State before the date of filing of the patent application or, if priority was claimed, before the date of priority, does in good faith an act which would constitute an infringement of the patent if it were then in force, or makes in good faith effective and serious preparations to do such an act, shall have the rights specified in s 55(2).

The rights referred to in s 55(2) are the following:

(a) the right to continue to do or, as the case may be, to do the act referred to in s 55(1);
(b) if such act was done or preparations had been made to so do it in the course of a business:
- in the case of an individual:
  - the right to assign the right to do it or to transmit such right on death, or
  - the right to authorise the doing of the act by any of his partners for the time being in the business in the course of which the act was done or preparations had been made to do it;
- in the case of a body corporate, the right to assign the right to do it or to transmit such right on the body's dissolution;

and the doing of that act by virtue of this subsection shall not amount to an infringement of the patent concerned.

There is no right to grant a licence.

Where a product which is the subject of a patent is disposed of by any person to another in exercise of a right conferred by s 55(2), that other and any person claiming through him shall be entitled to deal with the product in the same way as if it had been disposed of by a sole proprietor of the patent.

4.10.6 Right to continue use commenced while patent lapsed

Although a patent may lapse by reason of failure to pay renewal fees, s 37 of PA92 contains provisions for the restoration of the patent under certain circumstances. Section 37(7) provides that an order under the section for the restoration of a patent shall be subject to such provisions as are prescribed for the protection of persons who, during the period beginning on the date on which the patent lapsed and ending on the date of the order under the section, may have begun to avail themselves of the invention which is the subject of the patent. Rule 38 of PR92 prescribes the provisions for the protection of such persons.

4.10.7 Private use

Section 42(a) of PA92 provides that the rights conferred by a patent do not extend to acts done privately for non-commercial purposes.

4.10.8 Experimental use

Similarly, under s 42(b), an act done for experimental purposes relating to the subject matter of the relevant patented invention will not be an infringing act.

4.10.9 Extemporaneous preparation on prescription

Section 42(c) provides that the extemporaneous preparation for individual cases in a pharmacy of a medicine in accordance with a medical prescription issued by a registered medical practitioner or acts concerning the medicine so prepared do not infringe.

4.10.10 Vessels, vehicles and aircraft

4.10.10.1 Ships

The rights conferred by a patent do not extend to the use on board vessels registered in certain countries other than in the State of the invention which is the subject of the patent, in the body of the vessel, in the machinery, tackle, gear and other accessories, when such vessel temporarily or accidentally enters the territorial waters of the State, provided that the invention is used in such waters exclusively for the needs of the vessel.

4.10.10.2 Aircraft, hovercraft and vehicles

The rights conferred by a patent do not extend to the use of the invention which is the subject of the patent in the construction or operation of aircraft or land vehicles of certain countries other than the State or of such aircraft or land vehicle accessories when such aircraft or land vehicles temporarily or accidentally enter the State.

4.10.10.3 Breach of restrictive conditions

Section 83(4) states that the inclusion by the proprietor of a patent in a contract of any condition which by virtue of the section is null and void shall be available as a defence to an action for infringement of the patent to which the contract relates brought while that contract is in force.

Section 68(1) makes provision for the proprietor of a patent to apply to the Controller for an entry to be made in the register to the effect that licences under the patent are to be available as of right.

Section 68(2)(b) provides that where such an entry is made in the register then if in any proceedings for infringement of the patent (otherwise than by importation of goods) the defendant undertakes to take a licence on terms to be settled by the Controller, no injunction shall be granted against him. In addition, the amount (if any) recoverable against him by way of damages shall not exceed double the amount which would have been payable by him as licensee if such a licence had been granted before the earliest infringement.

4.11 Revocation

Section 57 of PA92 provides that any person may apply to the court or the Controller for revocation on the grounds set out in s 58. Section 57(5) provides that where there are proceedings with respect to a patent pending in the court under any provision of PA92, then the revocation application may not be made to the Controller without the leave of the court.

Section 59 gives power to the court or the Controller to revoke where they consider the grounds for revocation mentioned in s 58 prejudice the maintenance of the patent.

The grounds for revocation in s 58 are:

(a) that the subject matter of the patent is not patentable under PA92;
(b) the specification of the patent does not disclose the invention in a manner sufficiently clear and complete for it to be carried out by a person skilled in the art;
(c) there has been unlawful extension of the disclosure;
(d) the protection conferred by the patent has been extended by an amendment of the application or the specification of the patent;
(e) the proprietor of the patent is not entitled thereto.

Section 60 gives the power to the Controller to revoke patents on his own initiative.

If a European patent is under opposition at the EPO, a petition to revoke the same patent here may be stayed by the High Court because a decision by the EPO to revoke the patent would have automatic effect here under s 119(4) of PA92. Such a stay was granted by McCracken J in *Merck & Co Inc v GD Searle & Co* [2001] 2 ILRM 363 when the patent owners gave an undertaking not to enforce the patent by way of injunction pending final determination of the EPO.

4.12 Amendment

A reference to amendment is included so that a client may be advised in general terms as to the possibility of amending a patent application (s 32 of PA92) and amending the patent specification after grant (s 38 of PA92). The rules governing amendment distinguish between alterations in the description of the invention and in the claims. The description must not be amended so as to introduce matter extending beyond that disclosed in the specification as filed (s 32(2) and s 38(3) of PA92) and the claims must not be amended so as to extend the protection conferred by the patent (s 38(3) of PA92). If the claims are amended during application, they still have to satisfy the basic rule that they must be clear and concise and be supported by the description (s 20). Amendments which are wrongly admitted may provide a ground for revocation (s 58(c) and (d) of PA92). Where a specification is amended after grant under the provisions of s 38 the amendment is deemed always to have had effect from the date of grant of the patent. Amendment in the course of an application is frequent. Amendment after grant is much less frequent.

A patent specification defines the subject matter of the invention and by implication what people are free to do. Thus there is a public interest in applications for amendment after grant. This public interest is reflected in the fact that the intention to apply for amendment must be advertised (s 38(1) and (2) of PA92). In addition, s 38(5) provides that 'any person' may oppose the proposed amendment.

The onus on an applicant for amendment is heavy and he must make full disclosure to the court or the Controller as the case may be. Any undue delay in making application for amendment can be fatal.

Patent amendment has been a problem in the UK and Ireland for several years. Amendment remained a discretionary matter, effectively requiring the patentee to make full disclosure of all relevant materials – even those that were privileged. Despite attempts by lower courts in the UK to ease the position, the Court of Appeal in the UK reaffirmed the court's wide discretion in *Kimberly-Clark v Procter & Gamble* [2000] RPC 422. The issue is of importance where litigation uncovers prior art which invalidates certain claims of the patent, but where the claims could be limited to overcome the prior art.

One of the changes agreed at the Munich Diplomatic Conference in Munich in November 2000 effectively overturns the problem in seeking amendment. The new Art 105a of the EPC allows a patentee to apply to the EPO at any time to limit the patent, providing the patent is not in opposition at that time. The examination will effectively only be on formalities and is expected to go through quickly. When the revised EPC enters into force, this will provide a valuable, pan-European, mechanism for the rapid amendment of claims.

In addition, the new Art 138(3) of the EPC makes it clear that patentees will have a right to limit the claims of their patents in any proceedings before national courts where validity of the patent is in issue. The court would no longer appear to be able to exercise any discretion in the matter.

4.13 Remedy for groundless threats

Section 53 of PA92 has relevance when you are consulted by a client who owns a patent which he believes is being infringed and he requests you write to the alleged infringer or where you are consulted by a client who has received a cease and desist letter from a patent owner alleging he is infringing a patent. The purpose of the section is to give to a person who receives a threat of infringement proceedings a remedy to prevent the threats. It has long been recognised that a potential plaintiff can do damage by merely threatening to sue. A manufacturer or importer is particularly prone to damage where their customers are threatened and they capitulate to those threats.

Under s 53, if any person (whether or not entitled to any right in a patent) by circulars, advertisements or otherwise threatens another person with proceedings for any infringement of a patent, a person aggrieved by the threats (whether or not the person to whom the threats are made) may bring proceedings against the person making the threats, provided that proceedings may not be brought for a threat to bring proceedings for infringement alleged to consist of making or importing a product for disposal or of using a process. If the threats and the plaintiff's status as a person aggrieved are proved then the plaintiff can obtain relief unless the defendant proves that the acts in respect of which proceedings were threatened constitute or would constitute an infringement of a patent and the patent alleged to be infringed is not shown by the plaintiff to be invalid. The plaintiff may claim relief by way of a declaration, injunction and damages. Mere notification of the existence of a patent does not constitute a threat of proceedings within the meaning of s 53.

4.14 Declaration of non-infringement

The Oireachtas recognised that the threat of patent infringement proceedings is an exceptional hindrance to trade and s 54 of PA92 is a specific statutory provision enabling a third party to seek declarations of non-infringement from the court. This is so regardless of whether the patentee has made any assertion of infringement. By this procedure, third parties know where they stand before launching a new product or venture. The applicant must show that he has applied in writing to the proprietor or licensee for a written acknowledgment, the effect of which, if given, would be similar to that of the declaration claimed, and has furnished him with full particulars in writing of the process or product in question and the proprietor or licensee has refused or neglected to give such an acknowledgment.

The validity of a patent in whole or in part may not be called into question in proceedings for a declaration of non-infringement, and accordingly the making or refusal of such a declaration in the case of a patent shall not be deemed to imply that the patent is valid.

4.15 The role of a patent agent in patent litigation

A patent agent usually works with solicitors and counsel during patent litigation, in order to assist, *inter alia*:

(a) in interpreting the patent and investigating its validity;
(b) in providing background information about the technical field;
(c) in liaising with expert witnesses;
(d) in explaining specialist areas of patent law and practice, including European law and EPO practice;
(e) in participating in a 'confidentiality club' if evidence is made available to professional advisers only.

If a patent is found to be partially invalid and/or is amended during the litigation, the patent agent who drafted the original specification may be required to give evidence to satisfy the court that the specification was framed in good faith and with reasonable skill and knowledge.

4.16 Miscellaneous matters

4.16.1 Privileged communications of solicitors and patent agents

Section 94 of PA92 extends privilege to certain specified communications. A communication to which the section applies is privileged from disclosure in any proceedings (including a proceeding before the Controller or competent authority under the EPC or the PCT) to the same extent as a communication between client and solicitor is privileged in any proceedings before a court in the state. The section applies to a communication between a person (or a person acting on his behalf) and a solicitor or patent agent (or a person acting on his behalf) or for the purpose of obtaining, or in response to a request for, information which a person is seeking for the purpose of instructing a solicitor or patent agent in relation to any matter concerning the protection of an invention, patent, design or technical information or any matter involving passing off.

Under s 106(7) of PA92, nothing in this Act shall be construed as prohibiting solicitors from taking such part in proceedings under this Act as has heretofore been taken by solicitors in connection with a patent or any procedure relating to a patent or the obtaining thereof.

4.16.2 Action for disclosure

A person may be made a defendant in an action brought specifically to obtain discovery of the identity of infringers where that person (whether knowingly or not) 'has got mixed up in the tortious acts of others so as to facilitate their wrongdoing' (*Norwich Pharmacal Co v Customs & Excise Commissioners* [1974] AC 133). The costs of the innocent defendant in providing such information will be borne by the plaintiff, as will the costs of proceedings if the defendant properly doubts whether he should have to provide such information and submits the matter for determination by the court. The plaintiff may, however, be able to recover such costs from the infringer in subsequent proceedings.

The court has jurisdiction to order the disclosure of the name of a wrongdoer outside the jurisdiction even though such wrong-doing is under the laws of another country, provided it is shown that the transaction in which the defendant and the wrong-doer were involved related to the same subject matter (*Smith Kline & French Laboratories Ltd v Global Pharmaceuticals Ltd* [1986] RPC 394).

4.16.3   Customs & Excise procedure

Council Regulation EC/3295/94 concerns procedures for requesting national Customs Authorities to detain counterfeit or pirated goods. The procedures governed by this Regulation are in use in Ireland. However, this Regulation did not cover goods that infringed a patent.

Council Regulation EC/241/99 amends Regulation 3295/94 in a number of respects particularly by adding goods that infringe a patent to those goods that can be detained. The procedure involves notifying the Customs & Excise authorities of details of the right being infringed and details of the import or export of the relevant goods together with a request that the goods be detained. The applicant must also give a full written indemnity to the Customs & Excise authorities with regard to the detention of the goods. SI 1996/48 implemented the Regulation in Ireland.

CHAPTER 5

COPYRIGHT 1: THE COPYRIGHT AND RELATED RIGHTS ACT 2000

Rosaleen Byrne

5.1 Introduction and overview

The purpose of this chapter is to provide an introduction to and an overview of the Copyright and Related Rights Act 2000 (the 2000 Act). This will be done by setting the Act in context in European and international law developments and by outlining the extent to which those developments have shaped the Act. In addition, this chapter aims to highlight in what respects the 2000 Act introduces new concepts into Irish law, which depart from the law relating to copyright as set out in the Copyright Act 1963. Further, this chapter will address some of the basic building blocks of copyright law, namely the concepts of authorship, ownership, the nature and scope of copyright and the duration of copyright as it applies to various different works. The purpose of this latter part of the chapter is to provide a basis for more detailed chapters on specific aspects of copyright law and in particular Chapter 6 on infringement of copyright and enforcement of rights.

5.1.1 Setting the scene

Prior to the Act becoming effective on 1 January 2001, the law in Ireland relating to copyright was set out in the Copyright Act 1963 complemented by Irish case law relating to the application of the 1963 Act. Only four significant amendments to the 1963 Act were made prior to the adoption of the 2000 Act. These were as follows:

(a) a statutory instrument (SI 1995/158) implementing the Term Directive (Directive 93/98/EEC): the most important effect of this was to enhance the period of protection of copyright from the life of the author plus 50 years to the life of the author plus 70 years;

(b) the introduction by way of statutory instrument (SI 1993/26) of the Software Directive (Directive 91/250/EEC) providing copyright protection to computer programs as literary works in whatever form the program exists (including source code and object code);

(c) the provision of higher fines and terms of imprisonment in relation to offences committed under the 1963 Act, in the Intellectual Property (Miscellaneous Provisions) Act 1998 (in or around 1997 the US threatened to commence proceedings before the World Trade Organisation (WTO) if Ireland did not take steps to introduce more effective laws in relation to combating piracy in accordance with its obligations under the WTO Agreement on Trade Related Aspects of Intellectual Property Rights (TRIPS) and the 1998 Act was introduced in response to this threat);

(d) the introduction of legislation to address the conundrum of copyright subsisting in drawings (as artistic works) relating to spare parts and the anti-competitive effects of same, by the Copyright (Amendment) Act 1987.

It is clear that these important developments, which took place between 1963 and the adoption of the 2000 Act, related to very specific issues. It is also true to say that, in relation to three of these four issues, Ireland was coming under pressure either from the European Union or from the US to introduce legislation to comply with various treaty obligations. Notwithstanding these amendments, however, copyright legislation in Ireland as it existed prior to the adoption of the 2000 Act required a major overhaul. One reason for the overhaul was to ensure that Ireland changed its copyright law to reflect other obligations arising from international treaties and European harmonisation measures as outlined in more detail below. Another reason was the general requirement to modernise Irish copyright law to facilitate its application to modern technologies.

5.1.2 European Community (EC) law obligations

The driving force behind initiatives taken by the European Commission relating to intellectual property was the achievement of the objective of harmonising laws in the Community with a view to completing the internal market. It was clear from an early stage that intellectual property rights, given the fact that they confer a form of exclusive or monopolistic right, often relating to a specific territory, could be used to divide the internal market contrary to the general objectives of the Treaty of Rome in relation in particular to EC competition law principles (Art 81 and Art 82 (formerly Arts 85 and 86)).

Directorate General XV (DG XV), now known as the Market Directorate, was responsible for draft legislation in the area of harmonising intellectual property rights at Community level. This process commenced in 1988 with the publication by the Commission of its Green Paper on *Copyright and the Challenge of Technology – Copyright Issues Requiring Immediate Action*. A number of specific legislative acts were introduced subsequent to this Green Paper. These are as follows:

(a) **Directive 91/250/EEC on the legal protection of computer software programs**

This Directive, commonly known as the 'Software Directive', granted protection to computer programs as literary works, irrespective of the form in which the programs existed. Prior to the adoption of this Directive, there was a considerable amount of case law, particularly in common law jurisdictions, regarding whether or not computer programs (which in object code form consist merely of a number of electronic, non-human readable instructions to the processing unit of a computer) could be protected as a form of copyright. In many jurisdictions the courts struggled with trying to apply the traditional concepts of copyright to this form of work, while at the same time acknowledging that sufficient originality and effort went into creating computer programs to justify their protection. This Directive stated that computer programs are literary works and are to be protected as such under copyright law. This Directive was initially implemented in Irish law by way of statutory instrument in 1993 (SI 1993/26), which was subsequently replaced by Pt II of the 2000 Act. This Directive and its implementation into Irish law will be dealt with in more detail in Chapter 7.

(b) **Directive 92/100/EEC on rental rights and lending rights and on certain rights relating to copyright in the field of intellectual property**

This Directive is commonly referred to as the 'Rental and Lending Directive'. This Directive granted authors of copyright protected works exclusive rights to authorise the rental and lending of those works. This provides authors of protected works with a new form of right (ie, a new restricted act which they can prevent others from carrying out in relation to their work). It should be noted that the Directive does not apply to all works; eg, it does not apply to buildings or industrial designs. The Directive as it relates to rental and lending rights is implemented by virtue of s 42 of the 2000 Act. This Directive also deals with matters relating to neighbouring rights with a view to harmonising legislation relating to neighbouring rights.

(c) **Directive 93/83/EEC on the co-ordination of certain rules concerning copyright and rights relating to copyright applicable to satellite broadcasting and cable re-transmission**

This Directive provides authors with a right to communicate works to the public by satellite broadcast and it includes a number of provisions regulating this right. In addition, the Directive contains provisions ensuring that, where this act of communication to the public takes place in a third country (ie, a non-EU country), rules relating to the existence of these rights cannot be avoided within the Community. The Directive also deals with the issue of cable re-transmission.

The provisions of this Directive relating to satellite broadcasting are implemented by s 6 of the 2000 Act and the provisions relating to cable re-transmission are implemented by s 174 of the 2000 Act.

(d) **Directive 93/98/EEC harmonising the term of protection of copyright and certain related rights**

This Directive is commonly referred to as the 'Term Directive'. As stated above, it lengthens the period of protection available for certain works from the life of the author plus 50 years to the life of the author plus 70 years. This lengthened protection relates to copyright in literary and artistic works. The Directive also outlines the duration of neighbouring rights and the duration of rights in relation to other types of works, eg, films, sound recordings and computer generated works. This Directive was implemented by statutory instrument in Ireland in 1995, which is now replaced by ss 24–36 of the 2000 Act.

(e) **Directive 96/9/EC on the legal protection of databases**

This Directive is commonly referred to as the 'Database Directive' and while it recognises that copyright protection can be afforded to some databases/compilations (referred to as 'original databases'), where an originality test is satisfied, it also introduces a new right known as the *sui generis* database right. This *sui generis* right protects a database or compilation on the basis that the creation of these works require the investment of resources (financial, human and otherwise) and as a result they should benefit from some form of protection. The *sui generis* right entitles the owner of the right to prevent the unauthorised extraction and/or re-utilisation of the contents of the database. This right is referred to in ss 320–61 of the 2000 Act, and is dealt with in detail in Chapter 7.

5.1.3 Further developments at European Community level

At the time of adoption by the Irish legislature of the 2000 Act, a proposal for a new Directive on Copyright and Related Rights in the Information Society was being considered at EU level. As the title suggests, this proposal for a Directive was intended to deal with the creation and distribution of copyright works in different technologically advanced forms. In particular, it was intended to address issues arising from the exploitation of the internet by rights owners and users of protected works.

This Directive (Directive 01/29/EC of the European Parliament and of the Council on the harmonisation of certain aspects of copyright and related rights in the Information Society) has now been adopted and Member States were required to implement its provisions by 22 December 2002. Notwithstanding the fact that this Directive was proceeding through the legislative channels at European Level and would, in due course, be required to be implemented in Ireland, the passing of the Copyright and Related Rights Act 2000 was not delayed in order to give effect to the requirements of the Directive. At the time of writing this chapter, the Department of Enterprise, Trade and Employment in Ireland is considering the extent to which the 2000 Act requires amendment in order to give effect to this Directive. It is not envisaged that the adoption of this Directive will require significant changes to Irish legislation.

5.1.4 International treaty obligations

Ireland is a signatory to the Berne Convention for the Protection of Literary and Artistic Works, the most recent version of which is the Paris Act 1971. In addition, Ireland has certain obligations as a result of the conclusion of the GATT/TRIPS Agreement of 1993. It was as a result of this agreement that Ireland was pressured into adopting the Intellectual Property (Miscellaneous Provisions) Act 1998 to provide greater protection against piracy.

In the early 1990s, the World International Property Organisation (WIPO) had commenced work on a protocol to the Berne Convention, Paris Act 1971. This work culminated in the adoption of two treaties known as the WIPO Copyright Treaty (WCT) and the WIPO Phonograms and Performers Treaty (WPPT) adopted in December 1996 by a WIPO conference. These Treaties go a considerable way to addressing technological advances in the area of copyright protection and rights management and, in advance of being required to do so under EU law, Ireland took the initiative to introduce provisions in the 2000 Act to give effect to these aspects of the Treaties. (In this regard, see ss 370–76 of the 2000 Act relating to rights protection measures and rights management information and also s 40 relating to the so-called 'making available' right.)

As a result of Ireland's membership of the Berne Union and its most recent version, the Paris Act 1971, Ireland is obliged to provide for moral rights. This was a long outstanding obligation which had not been addressed by Ireland; however, it is now dealt with principally in ss 107–19 of the 2000 Act.

5.1.5 Modernising the law

A number of provisions in the 2000 Act are aimed at modernising the law in relation to copyright, and by doing so the provisions recognise the technologically advanced environments within which copyright works are created and exploited. By way of example the following provisions in particular should be noted:

(a) Section 39: this section outlines what is meant by the term 'copying' and it makes it clear that storing a work in 'any medium' and making copies of works which are 'transient' or 'incidental' to some other use of the work as in fact constitute copying (see, however, s 87, which contains an exception to this).

(b) Section 40: this section relates to the so-called 'making available' right. This section gives the owner of a copyright work a right to make available to the public copies of the work by wire or wireless means in such a way that members of the public may access the work from a place and at a time chosen by them (including the making available of copies of works through the internet). This section is intended to introduce a new right, whereby rightholders can control the making available of their works over the internet. This section is also intended to cover 'on demand' services such as video on demand, music on demand, etc.

Section 40(3) and subsequent subsections deal with the position of service providers acting as mere conduits for making available copies of a work to the public. In essence, these subsections are intended to ensure that intermediaries, such as internet service providers, are not liable for the making available of copyright works in an unauthorised manner (ie, infringement of copyright works) where they have only made provision for facilities to make the works available. This exception is subject to a requirement that, once a person who provides such facilities is notified by the owner of the copyright in a work concerned that the facilities are being used to infringe the copyright, that person has an obligation to remove the infringing material as soon as practical or else be liable for infringement. These provisions mirror the 'notice and take down' procedure of the Digital Millennium Copyright Act 2000 in the US.

(c) Sections 80–82: these sections, among others, relate to the legal protection of computer programs and replace the statutory instrument, which implemented the Software Directive into Irish law.

(d) Section 87: this section refers to transient or incidental copying and it is aimed at ensuring that the mere caching of copyright protected material on one's hard drive does not constitute an infringement of copyright. This section simply states that the making of a transient or incidental copy of a work, which is technically required for the viewing of or listening to the work by a member of the public to whom a copy of the work is made lawfully available, does not constitute an infringement of the work.

(e) Sections 370–74: these sections deal with devices, which are designed to circumvent rights protection technologies and find their origin in the WIPO Treaties of 1996 referred to above.

(f) Sections 375–76: these sections deal with rights management information and they introduce new offences regarding unlawful acts relating to the removal of or interference with rights management information. These sections also have their origins in the 1996 WIPO Treaties.

5.1.6 Summary

In summary, we can see that the main drivers behind the introduction of this legislation were Ireland's EC and international law obligations together with the general requirement to update the law to deal with technological advances as regards creating and exploiting copyright works.

If asked to identify the most significant changes introduced by the Act, it is suggested that the following are among the most important:

(a) the introduction of the database right for the first time in Ireland;
(b) the introduction of moral rights for the first time in Ireland;
(c) the general updating of Irish copyright law to deal with the Information Society.

Now that we have looked at the background to the introduction of the Act and the factors which shaped the Act, we will move on to consider some basic concepts of copyright law.

5.2 Basic concepts of copyright law

5.2.1 Nature of copyright

Section 17 of the 2000 Act sets out in broad terms the meaning of copyright as a form of protection and this section also outlines the different types of work in which copyright can subsist. Section 17(1) states:

> Copyright is a property right whereby, subject to this Act, the owner of the copyright in any work may undertake or authorise other persons in relation to that work to undertake certain acts in the State, being acts which are designated by this Act, as acts, restricted by copyright in a work of that description.

It is very important to note that copyright is described as a property right. This is relevant as regards licensing and assigning copyright and it also has a bearing on stamp duty issues.

In addition, it can be seen from s 17(1) that the right which copyright confers is a right to undertake certain restricted acts. The acts restricted by copyright in a work or, in other words, the rights of a copyright owner are set out in ss 37–43 of the 2000 Act. If restricted acts are carried out by a third party who has not been authorised to carry out those acts by or on behalf of the copyright owner, then this will constitute an infringement of copyright. Sections 37–43 of the Act set out what constitutes an infringement of copyright. In addition, ss 44–48 of the Act set out what are known as secondary infringements. Restricted acts, and primary and secondary infringement, will be dealt with in Chapter 6. However, for the present purposes, one should note that copyright confers on the owner of the copyright the exclusive right to carry out restricted acts subject to certain exceptions.

We will now turn to consider the different categories of works in which copyright can subsist.

5.2.2 Copyright works

Copyright can subsist in:

(a) original literary, dramatic, musical or artistic works;
(b) sound recordings, films, broadcasts or cable programmes;
(c) the typographical arrangement of published editions;
(d) original databases.

Copyright will only subsist in a work if the requirements for copyright protection specified in the Act with respect to qualification are complied with.

Sections 182–90 (Chapter 18) of the 2000 Act deal with qualification for copyright protection. Certain requirements must be satisfied in relation to the author, country, territory, state or area in which the work seeking copyright protection was first lawfully made available to the public before copyright can subsist in a work. Although s 17 of the Act sets out the instances where copyright would subsist in works, this is with the proviso (s 17(4) of the 2000 Act) that such a work complies with the qualification requirements set out in Chapter 18 of the 2000 Act. While these qualifications refer to the author and the geographical area where the work was made, it is not clear from s 18(2) whether or not the requirements are alternatives or are cumulative. The general view, having regard to the equivalent English legislation and the terms of the Berne Convention, is that the requirements are alternatives. These qualification criteria effectively limit qualification for the rights in question under Irish law to materials protected by corresponding laws in countries with which Ireland shares obligations under international law, and in this regard the Berne Convention is of particular relevance.

It is critical to understand that copyright protection does not extend to ideas, which underlie a particular work; rather it is the expression of an idea, which copyright protects. This is reflected in s 17(3) of the Act, which states:

> Copyright protection shall not extend to the ideas and principles which underlie any element of a work, procedures, methods of operation or mathematical concepts ...

The practical effect of this can be demonstrated with a simple example. If a computer programmer has a new idea for an innovative piece of software, but does not actually write the code for the software or express the idea in any written or recorded manner, then if another computer programmer comes up with the same idea, either independently or through having heard of the idea, and writes the software code to give expression to the idea, then the computer programmer who had the original idea cannot take any action on the basis of copyright against the second programmer. It should be noted that depending on the circumstances surrounding the facts, the person with the original idea may have an action for breach of confidence against the person who ultimately uses the idea. Any such action, however, is based on equitable principles and is not a statutory right.

The categories of work set out at subpara (a) above, namely original, literary, dramatic, musical or artistic works, are amongst the most common works which are protected by copyright. Accordingly, it is proposed to take a closer look at this category of works. Before looking at each of these categories separately to see what they encompass, we should consider the meaning of the word 'original' in the context of copyright law. Depending on the facts, there may be an action for breach of confidence, but copyright will provide no assistance to the person with the original idea if it has not been expressed in some form.

It is important to bear this in mind in practice, as clients will often seek your advice on whether or not they can take action to prevent a third party from using their idea. Clients are often of the view that they can rely on copyright protection even where they have not committed their idea to some form of expression.

5.2.2.1 *Originality*

It is by now well-settled law that the word 'original' in the context of copyright law does not mean that the work must be the expression of original or inventive thought. Rather, it means original in the sense of not copied. The essential issue in copyright law is whether the person who claims copyright has independently created the work or merely copied the efforts of others. The judgment of Peterson J in the case of *University of London Press Ltd v University Tutorial Press Ltd* [1916] 2 Ch 601, at 608–09, is instructive in this regard:

> The word 'original' does not in this connection mean that the work must be the expression of original or inventive thought. Copyright Acts are not concerned with the originality of ideas, but with the expression of thought, and, in the case of 'literary work' with the expression of thought in print or writing. The originality which it requires relates to the expression of the thought. But the Act does not require that the expression must be in an original or novel form but that the work must not be copied from another work – that it should originate from the Author.

In the past, the issue of originality has most commonly arisen in the case of compilations. Compilations generally consist of a collection of existing works or facts, and the issue which arises is whether or not there has been sufficient exercise of labour, judgment or skill in the production of a compilation so as to satisfy the test of originality. Generally, even if a work is based on a pre-existing work, if there is skill involved in re-drafting, rephrasing, organising or reformatting the work, this could involve sufficient skill or judgment to make the resulting work an original work. This issue will be dealt with in more detail in the chapter relating to databases.

In the following sections, the terms 'literary, dramatic, musical and artistic works' are considered. It is not possible within the scope of this chapter to consider each of the different categories of work in which copyright can subsist. However, literary, dramatic, musical and artistic works are the most common works we come across in practice and these are discussed briefly below. Readers are referred to the annotated version of the 2000 Act

5.2.2.1.1 Literary work

The 2000 Act states that 'literary work' means a work, including a computer program but does not include a dramatic or musical work, or an original database which is written, spoken or sung. This is the only guidance that the Act gives as regards the meaning of the words 'literary work'.

One of the leading statements in relation to the meaning of the words 'literary work' was made by Peterson J again in the case of *University of London Press Ltd* (cited at section 5.2.2.1 above) where he said:

> In my view, the words 'literary work' cover work which is expressed in print or writing, irrespective of the question whether the quality or style is high. The word 'literary' seems to be used in a sense somewhat similar to the use of the word literature in political or electioneering literature and refers to written or printed matter.

We can see from the above that 'literary work' does not mean scholarly or learned works of literature, but rather it means a printed or written work. Section 18(1) of the Act reflects this as it states:

> Copyright shall not subsist in a literary, dramatic or musical work or in an original database until that work is recorded in writing or otherwise by a written consent of the author.

An issue, which has arisen in the past and which tests the scope of the expression 'literary work', is whether or not copyright subsists in the title of a book, a song or an advertising slogan. In some cases, it has been held that titles to songs are 'too insubstantial' to attract copyright in the title alone. The cases relating to this issue have looked at whether or not sufficient skill and judgment have been exercised to warrant something being held to be literary. In general, the selection of a title for a book or a song from common phrases or everyday words has been considered not to have involved exercising sufficient skill and judgment.

It is clear, therefore, that although the meaning of 'literary work' is very broad and is taken to mean written or printed material, rather than a scholarly work, some degree of skill or judgment must be exercised if a work is to be described as a literary work.

5.2.2.1.2 Dramatic work

The Act defines a dramatic work 'as including a choreographic work or a work of mime' (s 2 of the 2000 Act). In order to qualify for protection under the Act dramatic works, like literary works, must be original. A dramatic work must be capable of being physically performed (*Norowzian v Arks Ltd* [1999] FSR 79) and action or movement by people appears to be a key element of a dramatic work. Therefore, words, music or props by themselves (while they may attract separate protection) are not sufficient to constitute a dramatic work. It should also be noted that performance of a dramatic work may give rise to separate rights under Pt III of the Act relating to performers' rights.

5.2.2.1.3 Musical works

A musical work is defined in s 2 of the 2000 Act as:

> ... a work consisting of music, but does not include any words, or action, intended to be sung, spoken or performed with the music.

Therefore, the music of a song will enjoy copyright protection as a musical work, and separate literary copyright or dramatic copyright may attach the song as a whole.

5.2.2.1.4 Artistic works

Artistic works are defined in s 2 of the 2000 Act as including:

> ... a work of any of the following descriptions irrespective of their artistic quality:
>
> (a) photographs, paintings, drawings, diagrams, maps, charts, plans, engravings, etchings, lithographs, wood cuts, prints or similar works, collages or sculptures (including any cast or model made for the purposes of a sculpture);
>
> (b) works of architecture, being either buildings or models for buildings; and
>
> (c) works of artistic craftsmanship.

This, however, is not an exhaustive definition and it should be viewed in this light. It is clear from this definition that artistic merit or aesthetic value is not necessary for qualification as an artistic work.

5.2.2.2 Authorship

Authorship and ownership of copyright need to be considered as two separate concepts. Although these concepts are linked, due to the provision that the author of a work is the first owner of copyright in the work, it is often the case in relation to works of commercial value that the original author is generally not the party who ultimately owns and exploits the copyright.

Section 21 of the 2000 Act states that the 'author' means 'the person who creates a work'. Section 21 then goes on to give a list of certain persons who are included within the definition of author for specific classes of works. By way of example, s 21 states that author, in the case of a sound recording, includes the producer and in the case of a film includes the producer and the principal director. Other categories of note are computer-generated works in which case the person by whom the arrangements necessary for the creation of the work are undertaken is an author, and in the case of a photograph the photographer is an author.

There has been some criticism of the drafting of this section of the legislation in particular as the wording of this section leaves it open for other people to be included as an author. For example, in the case of a film, the Act states that 'author' means the person who creates the work, and includes the producer and the principal director. It might be possible, therefore, for another party who has had a significant input into the creation of the film to claim that they are also an author of the film. Clearly, from a commercial point of view, this could give rise to difficulties in ascertaining who the author of the work is and who is entitled to exploit the rights in a work. This is important because, as a general rule, the author of a work is the first owner of copyright in that work. Accordingly, it would seem prudent that where parties have an input or involvement in the creation of a work, they should be specifically requested to waive any claim to authorship in respect of the work if the absence of such a waiver could lead to complicating circumstances. Section 22 of the 2000 Act deals with works of joint authorship.

5.2.2.3 Ownership

Section 23(1) of the 2000 Act sets out the general rule that the author of a work shall be the first owner of the copyright. This section goes on to set out four exceptions to this general principle. The exception which practitioners come across most often, in practice, is that when a work is made by an employee in the course of employment, the employer is the first owner of any copyright in the work, subject to any agreement to the contrary. This is the main exception set out to the general rules.

Section 23(2) of the 2000 Act contains a specific rule relating to authors of works who are employed by proprietors of newspapers or periodicals. This section states:

> Where a work, other than a computer program, is made by an author in the course of employment by a proprietor of a newspaper or periodical, the author may use the work for any purpose, other than for the purpose of making available that work to newspapers or periodicals, without infringing the copyright in the work.

This section was the subject of intense debate at all stages of the Bill and it was argued by the National Newspapers of Ireland that these residual rights of employed journalists should be omitted on the grounds that they potentially allowed an employed journalist to undermine his employer in the market place by using his rights in other media such as television or radio. According to the relevant Minister at the time, the final text was intended to be a reasonable and honourable compromise between competing interests.

5.2.2.4 Duration of a copyright

The duration of copyright depends on the type of work being considered. Sections 24–30 of the 2000 Act set out the duration of copyright in various different types of work. Set out below are the main categories of works and the duration of copyright relating to these.

(a) Literary, dramatic, musical and artistic works or original databases – copyright expires 70 years after the death of the author, irrespective of the date in which the work is first lawfully made available to the public. In the event of any of the above works being anonymous or pseudonymous, copyright will expire 70 years after the date on which the work was first lawfully made available to the public.

(b) Copyright in a film will expire 70 years after the last of the following people dies:
- the principal director of the film;
- the author of the screenplay of the film;
- the author of the dialogue of the film;
- the author of music specifically composed for use in the film.

(c) Copyright in sound recording expires 50 years after the sound recording is made or, if first lawfully made available to the public during this 50 years, after the date of such making available.

(d) Copyright in a broadcast will expire 50 years after the broadcast was first lawfully transmitted.

(e) Copyright in a work which is computer generated will expire 70 years after the date in which the work is first lawfully made available to the public.

There are a number of other miscellaneous provisions relating to the duration of copyright contained in Pt I, Chapter 3 of the 2000 Act and these should be considered in detail if advising on an issue regarding the duration of copyright.

5.2.3 The scope of copyright protection: restricted acts

Section 37(1) of the 2000 Act sets out the acts which are restricted by copyright in a work, ie, the acts which the right holder has the exclusive right to do or to authorise others to do. These acts are as follows:

(a) to copy the work;
(b) to make available to the public the work;

(c) to make an adaptation of the work or to undertake any of the acts referred to in (a) or (b) in relation to an adaptation.

These rights are addressed in further detail in the provisions which follow s 37 of the Act. In particular:

- s 39 deals with the reproduction right;
- s 40 deals with the making available right;
- s 41 deals with the distribution right;
- s 42 deals with the rental and lending right; and
- s 43 deals with adaptations.

These rights are subject to the exceptions set out in Chapter 6 of the Act and are also subject to the licensing provisions (see generally s 38, Chapter 8 and Chapter 16 of the Act). The exceptions are dealt with in detail in Chapter 6 of this text.

It is an infringement to undertake any of the foregoing acts restricted by copyright or to authorise another to undertake any of the foregoing without the permission of the copyright owner (s 37(2) of the 2000 Act). Infringement can occur with respect to a substantial part of the work as well as to the whole of the work (s 37(3) of the 2000 Act). What constitutes 'substantial' is a question of fact and will differ in each case. In the case of *Ladbroke v William Hill* [1964] 1 WLR 237, the Court of Appeal held that whether or not the amount copied is substantial is a matter of quality rather than quantity. Accordingly, a person who only copies a small portion of a work may, nonetheless, be found to have infringed copyright. In this case, the court also stated that the reproduction of part of a work that is not original will not normally constitute a substantial part of the work.

Furthermore, although innocent infringement is no defence (*Mansell v Valley Printing Co* [1908] 2 Ch 441) where a court is satisfied that at the time of the infringement the defendant 'did not know and had no reason to believe' copyright subsisted in the relevant work, then no damages will be awarded. In those circumstances, other remedies such as injunctions or delivery up of infringing materials are still available to the plaintiff.

It is important to bear in mind, in proving that there has been an infringement of the right of the copyright owner, a plaintiff will have to show that the defendant copied the plaintiff's work and that the work produced is similar or identical to the plaintiff's work. An infringement cannot occur if a work was independently created. In addition an infringing act can be undertaken directly or indirectly; therefore, it is irrelevant whether the work was copied directly or some other medium was used.

In *Computer Associates v Altai* [1992] 23 IPR 385, the court set out a four-pronged test to be applied in determining whether an infringement has taken place. The elements of this test are as follows:

(a) Is the plaintiff's work protected by copyright?
(b) Are there similarities between the plaintiff's and the defendant's work?
(c) Are there similarities as a result of copying?
(d) If copying is found, does it constitute a substantial part of the plaintiff's work?

In practice, a further question may be added which is:

(e) Does the Act come within any of the exemptions set out in Chapter 6 of the Act?

We will now move on to consider the more detailed provisions of the Act in relation to these restricted acts.

5.2.3.1 Reproduction right

Section 39 of the 2000 Act sets out the scope of the 'reproduction right', which as we have seen is one of the restricted acts. Section 39(2) states:

> There shall be a right of the owner of copyright to copy a work or to authorise others to do so which shall be known and in this part referred to as the 'Reproduction Right'.

Section 39(1) explains that copying shall be construed as including references, in relation to literary work, as storing the work in any medium and making copies of the work which are transient or incidental to some other use of the work. This subsection also explains what copying means in relation to other types of works.

5.2.3.2 'Making available' right

Section 40 sets out what is covered by this right. Most significantly, this right includes the making available to the public of copies of the works, by wire or wireless means, in such a way that members of the public may access the work from a place and at a time chosen by them (including making available of copies of work through the internet). This right also includes performing, showing or playing a copy of the work in public, broadcasting a copy of the work, and renting and lending copies of the work to the public.

Section 40 provides that the copyright owner has the exclusive right to undertake or authorise others to make copies of a work available to the public. This section also deals with the liability of intermediaries such as service providers. This issue was addressed in 5.1.5 of this chapter, where certain provisions of the Act which relate to technological advances were discussed. In addition, the making available right is based on Art 8 of the WIPO Copyright Treaty.

5.2.3.3 Distribution right

Section 41 confers a distribution right on the right holder. The right to issue or publish works to the public is part of the 'making available' right under s 40 and is also covered by the distribution right in s 41. This right is described as the right of a copyright owner to issue copies of a work to the public or to authorise others to do so.

This section explains that the 'issue of copies of a work to the public' can be construed as including the act of putting into circulation in a Member State of the European Economic Area (EEA) copies not previously put into circulation in the EEA, by or with the licence of the copyright owner; or the act of putting into circulation, outside Member States of the EEA, copies not previously put into circulation in a Member State of the EEA or elsewhere.

The right to issue works is subject to the Community doctrine of exhaustion, which provides that, once a work has been made available in a Member State of the EEA, the right holder cannot prevent further distribution within the EEA. Distribution outside the EEA may, however, be prevented and the right holder can prevent the importation of works into the EEA, from countries outside the EEA. This is reflected in s 41(2).

5.2.3.4 Rental and lending rights

Section 42 specifically states that there shall be a right of the owner to rent copies of a work or to authorise others to do so, which shall be known as the 'rental right', and there shall also be a right of the owner of copyright to lend copies of a work or to authorise others to do so, which shall be known as the 'lending right'. The rights apply in respect to literary, dramatic, musical and artistic works (except building or models of buildings), original databases, sound recording and typographical arrangements.

The distinction between rental and lending is as follows:

- Rental involves an economic or commercial advantage accruing to the right holder and it involves the work being returned after a period of time.
- Lending on the other hand does not involve an economic or commercial advantage accruing to the right holder and it can be done through a public establishment such as a library.
- Rental or lending under the Act is for private purposes and specifically excludes the performance, playing or showing in public of a work (which acts are covered by a making available right in s 40).

5.2.3.5 Secondary infringement of copyright

Sections 44–48 of the 2000 Act deal with secondary infringements of copyright. The purpose of these sections is to make unlawful ancillary acts such as dealing in or assisting in infringements carried out by other persons. Under these sections, it is illegal to import infringing copies, to possess or deal with infringing copies in a commercial sense, to permit the use of premises for infringing performances or to provide apparatus for infringing performances. In order for secondary infringement to occur, the alleged infringer must know or have had reason to believe that an infringement has taken place.

The issues which arise on infringement and in particular issues relating to enforcement of rights will be dealt with in Chapter 6.

CHAPTER 6

COPYRIGHT 2: THE ENFORCEMENT OF COPYRIGHT

Garrett Breen

6.1 Introduction

The protection of copyright in Ireland has in recent years been a matter of great concern for the Irish government. The Copyright and Related Rights Act 2000 (the 2000 Act) and the enforcement remedies contained within it were the result of a lengthy political process.

During the drafting of the Act, the government (especially Mary Harney, the relevant Minister at the time) came under pressure from both Europe and the US. In Europe, there was a feeling that Ireland was lagging behind the implementation of the World Trade Organisation Agreement on Trade Related Aspects of Intellectual Property Rights (TRIPS) and from the US side, there was pressure from the software industry in particular to make sure that any amended laws would be strong on software piracy. There had been some misconceptions about the proofs required in copyright infringement prosecutions in Ireland and the industry was trying to put this right and clarify some issues that were in doubt. Some of these misconceptions are mentioned later in this chapter.

6.2 Enforcement provisions in the 1963 Copyright Act (the 1963 Act)

Contrary to popular belief, the enforcement provisions in the 1963 Act were quite strong and although the 2000 Act has improved on these enforcement provisions there was not, in fact, too much to improve on. Under s 27(4) of the 1963 Act (as amended by the 1977 Copyright Act), application could be made to the District Court for an order to seize infringing goods. This was a very useful provision and was used by several sportswear and clothing manufacturers to combat the huge amount of counterfeiting that was taking place in Dublin (especially Henry Street) at the time as well as in other locations around the country such as the Ashford Market in Wicklow and in Letterkenny, Co Donegal.

Also, there was a misconception that under the 1963 Act, if one was bringing a prosecution for infringement of copyright, it was necessary to have the person who created the work in court to prove that he created the work and therefore owned the copyright in it. This necessity was finally put to bed in the 2000 Act. In fact it had already been decided in the case stated of *District Judge Martin* [1993] ILR 651 that it was not necessary to have the author of the copyright in court to give evidence at all.

6.3 Infringement

In order to consider what infringement of copyright entails, we must go back to the original definition of copyright which has been outlined in Chapter 5 ante. As previously outlined, copyright relates to certain restricted acts in relation to a work in which copyright subsists which are reserved to the copyright owner. In other words, these acts can only be done by the copyright owner. If they are to be done by someone else, they can only be done with the consent of the copyright owner, either through a licence or through an outright assignment of the copyright owner's rights. Essentially one can infringe copyright in a work if one undertakes one of the restricted acts without the consent of the copyright owner. In other words, if you make a copy of the work, make the work available to the public or make an adaptation of the work you will infringe.

In s 37(2) it is stated that:

> The copyright in a work is infringed by a person who without the licence of the copyright owner, undertakes, or authorises another to undertake, any of the Acts restricted by copyright.

6.4 Substantial part

Infringement can occur with respect to the entire work or indeed a substantial part of the work; but what constitutes a substantial part of the work? The case law would suggest that substantial relates to quality as well as quantity. These particular factors are more appropriate in relation to particular works, eg as regards a poem, either a substantial part of it is copied, word for word, or it is not.

However, in the case of a musical work for example, one work may have the characteristics qualitatively of another work while a lesser quantity of that work has been copied.

In *Ladbroke v William Hill* [1964] 1 WLR 273, the Court of Appeal held that whether an amount of work is taken is a question of quality rather than quantity. In *Coppinger and Scone James*, it states:

> Whether the defendant's work has been produced by the substantial use of those features of the plaintiff's work which, by reason of the knowledge, skill and labour employed in the production, constitute it an original copyright work, ie has the defendant made a substantial use of those features of the plaintiff's work in which copyright subsists? (*Krisarts SA v Briarfine Ltd* [1977] FSR 557).

In *Ricordi v Clayton and Waller Ltd* [1928] 35 MacCC 154, it was recognised that eight bars of a musical work might constitute a substantial part. As regards a musical work, there is not simply a question of note by note comparison and it falls to be determined not only by the eye but also by the ear.

The case of *Frances Day Hunter Ltd v Bron* [1963] 2 All ER 16 dealt with the copyright in musical works and the court outlined particular principles which were as follows:

(a) Reproduction of a work involves two elements:
- a sufficient objective similarity; and
- a causal connection between the two works, ie one being derived from the other.

(b) The causal connection may occur through:
- conscious copying by the defendant;
- unconscious copying where neither intention to infringe nor knowledge or infringement need be proven by the plaintiff.

A substantial degree of objective similarity gives rise to three possible explanations:
- conscious copying;
- unconscious copying;

- coincidence which may give rise to an inference of a causal connection and may thus shift the burden of proof to the defendant.
(c) Whether or not there was a causal connection is a question of fact which the court will determine upon the basis of the evidence before the court at the trial, especially the testimony of the composer of the allegedly infringing work.
(d) If the court accepts the denial of conscious copying, the evidence of the expert witnesses will be significant in the factual decision as to the existence of a causal connection.

In *Newspaper Licensing Agency Ltd v Marks & Spencer* [2000] 4 All ER 239, the plaintiff owned, by assignment, the copyright in the typographical arrangement of various national and regional newspapers in the UK. It brought proceedings against M & S for breach of that copyright as M & S provided a clipping service which delivered cuttings of items from newspapers of interest to M & S's business activities, to its staff. These were then distributed amongst the executives and staff of the company. The Court of Appeal held that since M & S was only cutting and copying small sections of an entire published newspaper, none of which amounted to a substantial part of the work, copyright of the plaintiff had not been infringed.

6.5 Innocent infringement

An innocent infringement is no defence. It only precludes the plaintiff from recovering damages. Section 128(2) of the 2000 Act states that:

> ... where in an action for infringement of the copyright in a work, it is shown that at the time of the infringement, the defendant did not know and had no reason to believe that copyright subsisted in the work to which the action relates, the plaintiff is not entitled to damages against the defendant.

6.6 Primary and secondary infringement

The primary infringement of a work in which copyright subsists takes place when one undertakes one of the restricted Acts, such as reproduction, making available, distribution, renting and lending and adapting the work. However, it is possible to undertake a secondary infringement. This consists of doing something with a copy of a work in which copyright subsists which is already an infringing copy.

It is unlawful to deal in or assist in infringements carried out by other persons. An infringing copy is a copy, the making of which would be an infringement of the copyright in the work concerned or the work is to be imported into the state and its making in the state would have been an infringement of the copyright in the work concerned or breach of an exclusive licence agreement relating to the work.

Section 44 of the 2000 Act excludes works as being infringing copies where the works are issued in accordance with the distribution right in another Member State of the European Economic Area (EEA).

However, the importation of a work which is not itself an infringing copy from outside the EEA without the permission of the right holder would be secondary infringement. Secondary infringement is set out in ss 45–48 of the 2000 Act. It is unlawful to import infringing copies, process or deal with infringing copies in the course of business, permit the use of premises for infringing performances or to provide an apparatus for infringing performances. However, in relation to all the secondary infringements, it is necessary for the person to have reason to believe that an infringement has taken place.

Two particular items of secondary infringement are discussed and analysed below.

6.6.1 Dealing with infringing copy

Section 45 states that a person infringes the copyright in a work where he without the licence of the copyright owner:

(a) sells, rents or lends or offers or exposes for sale, rental or loan;
(b) imports into the state, otherwise than for his private and domestic use;
(c) in the course of a business trade or profession has as in his possession, custody or control or makes available to the public; or
(d) otherwise than in the course of a business, trade or profession makes available to the public to such an extent as to prejudice the interest of the owner of the copyright;
(e) a copy of the work which is and which he knows or has reason to believe is an infringing copy of the work.

Therefore, the constituent element of the infringement is that the person infringing does not have the consent or the licence of the owner. If the person sells, rents or lends, it is implied that they are doing so in the course of a business. If they imported into the State (other than just bringing a few CDs home for their personal use), this is an infringement. If it is part of their business or they have mere possession, custody or control of the infringing works or outside of the course of business and make the copies available to the public to prejudice the interest of the owner of the copyright, this is an infringement.

A proviso allows the importation to the state for private and domestic use of an infringing copy. However, if the individual then (not as part of a business venture) distributes these CDs bought on holidays to their friends, that would be a secondary infringement.

6.6.2 Permitting use of premises for infringing performances

Section 47(1) states that where the copyright in a work is infringed by a performance at a place of public entertainment, any person who gave permission for that place to be used for the performance shall also be liable for the infringement unless, when that person gave permission, he had reason to believe that the performance would not infringe copyright.

In this section 'place of public entertainment' includes premises which are occupied mainly for other purposes and which are from time to time made available for hire for the purpose of public entertainment. There is a necessity for a plaintiff to prove in this instance that there was, in fact, an infringement.

The defence to such proceedings would be that when the owner of the premises gave permission, they did not honestly believe that the performance would infringe copyright. Interestingly, a place of public entertainment is defined to include such premises as temporary stages and temporary halls or marquees or any premises not normally used for entertainment, eg, for 'raves', but which are used for that purpose from time to time.

6.7 Remedies

There are a number of remedies available to the copyright owner and these can be divided into civil and criminal remedies. Within these divisions there are more immediate or interlocutory remedies as well as those more long term remedies.

6.7.1 Civil remedies

Section 127 of the Act states that an infringement of the copyright in a work is actionable by the copyright owner. The plaintiff therefore must be the person who owns the copyright, either by being the author or by having the copyright assigned to him. As copyright is a property right, the normal remedies of damages, injunctions and account of profits are available to the owner.

As regards proof of ownership, one has to look at s 139 in Chapter 12 of the Act which deals with the presumptions in relation to copyright. Under s 139, the presumptions apply to any proceedings whether civil or criminal for infringement of the copyright in any work. The Act states under s 139(2) that:

> Copyright shall be presumed to subsist in a work until the contrary is proved.

The software industry, in particular, was adamant that this presumption should be contained in the new Copyright Act. However, as mentioned above, it is likely that this presumption already existed and was a rebuttable presumption. Therefore, rather than the person who wrote the software having to come to court to prove the ownership of it, it is up to the alleged infringer to prove that they do not own it.

Again in s 139 as regards a book, CD or photograph, where a person is identified as the author or a joint author by name, statement, label or any other mark, there is also a presumption that the information is correct. In addition, under s 139, the plaintiff who owns copyright in a work through assignment or through the copyright being left to him by will, will not necessarily need to prove it.

6.7.1.1 A typical High Court infringement action

The following is an example of what typically would occur to a set of High Court proceedings in relation to the infringement of a musical copyright.

In this example a new band called 'Seven' has recorded an album which is about to be distributed to all of the record shops in Ireland and generally made available to the public. It is also about to be played on the various radio stations.

A long-established band known as 'Eight' hears a preview of the new album on an evening radio show hosted by DJ Rave Canning and is disgusted to find that the tune played bears an enormous resemblance to a tune on an album that they have had for some time.

There are still three days to go to the official launch and so the band manager and publisher go to the intellectual property lawyer. She writes an accusatory letter to the band and to its publishers accusing them of copying the work, pointing out that the album as published is an infringement of their copyright and calling upon them to undertake not to bring out the album or distribute it in any way. The letter also threatens an injunction if they fail to cease and desist the publication, etc. The letter states that if they do not undertake by close of business on a particular day, say that Friday, Eight will go into court to seek an injunction. With the letter is a draft letter for Seven to write on their own letterhead giving the undertakings. These undertakings also include an undertaking not to pass off the work, to deliver up all albums, etc.

In anticipation of Seven not 'caving in', the lawyers for Eight get ready for the injunction in any event. An undertaking not to publish is not forthcoming from Seven and so the relevant affidavits are sworn. In these affidavits, Eight's album is exhibited and a tape containing the broadcast on the radio is also exhibited.

Application is then made to the court *ex parte* and the judge listens to both tunes. The judge considers whether there is a stateable case and grants the interim injunction prohibiting the launch of the album until the following Monday morning. He directs that the injunction order be served by fax and orally to the publishers of the album and that letters also be sent to the distributor of the album as well as all the radio stations in the State where the album is to be played. The court papers including all the affidavits are then to be served on Seven and the motion is made returnable before the court on the following Monday morning. On Monday morning, the barristers for both sides meet and they discuss what will happen in the Monday morning motion list. It is agreed between the barristers that the matter be adjourned for another week and an undertaking is given by Seven to the court not to publish or perform the album.

When Seven has had a chance to file replying affidavits to the affidavits filed by Eight, there is a complete rehearing of the injunction application except that this time Seven's affidavit gives evidence as to how they contracted with a songwriter to write a song. He then wrote a song and gave it to them to record on their new album. There is an affidavit from the songwriter where he goes into great detail as to how he came up with the song in his attic and that his wife heard him singing it for the first time. There is also an affidavit from the wife.

After listening to the evidence, the court lifts the interlocutory injunction and reserves costs to the trial of the action.

Eight will continue on with their action. However, Eight will have to pay damages to Seven for the delay in the publication of their album under their undertaking as to damages.

When the matter comes for trial, the trial judge is very convinced by a musicologist who gives a very convincing report about the origins of the two songs and that they could not have come about as a coincidence. The judge upholds the plaintiff's case and awards damages.

6.7.2   Other civil remedies

6.7.2.1   Orders for delivery up and seizure

In the 2000 Act, new provisions were made for delivery up of infringing goods as well as for seizure of these infringing goods.

6.7.2.2   Order for delivery up

Under s 131 of the 2000 Act, where a person in the course of business has an infringing copy of a work, an article designed or adapted for making copies of a work or has a protection defeating device in their custody or control, it is possible for the owner of copyright in the work to apply to the appropriate court for an order that the article or device will be delivered up to him or to such other person as the court directs. Once the delivery up has occurred, the person to whom the work is delivered up has to comply with s 145 of the Act so that the goods delivered up can be forfeited to the copyright owner or destroyed or otherwise dealt with as the court directs. In considering its order, the court should consider what other remedies are available which will be adequate to compensate the copyright owner. If the court decides not to forfeit or destroy the goods, they are returned then to the person for whom they were seized.

Very often in these instances the copyright owner decides to give the goods to charity or to use them for some other purpose. However, experience shows that copyright owners are sometimes very reluctant to give these goods to charity as they tend to end up back in the hands of the infringer or counterfeiter. A popular charity, therefore, is the Prison Service as at least the goods are kept within a particular area!

Under s 132, if the District Court is satisfied that there are reasonable grounds for believing that infringing copies of the work, articles designed for making copies of the work and protection defeating devices are being hawked, carried about or marketed, upon application by the copyright owner to the court, he can order a member of the Garda Síochána to seize, without warrant, the copies, articles and devices and bring them before the District Court. When the court is satisfied that these articles are infringing copies, the District Court can order the copy, article or device to be destroyed or to be delivered up.

Under this particular section, the court can receive hearsay evidence to the effect that the witness or deponent believes that that material may be found in a particular location. The witness doesn't have to indicate the source of the information upon which they form a belief at this application. However, someone aggrieved by such an order can apply to the District Court for damages and the court can award damages if it establishes that there was no infringement and that the information was given maliciously. Again, this application is dealt with under s 132.

6.7.2.3 Difference between delivery up and seizure

The delivery up provision under s 131 is only of any use insofar as it will be met with a compliant infringer. If the infringer decides that he is not going to deliver up the goods, then the person serving the order must return to the court and seek an order for contempt. This is quite unsatisfactory as once the order for contempt is being sought and the solicitor has gone back to the infringer, all of the goods are probably disposed of at that stage. In these circumstances this kind of order is better used for an ordinary shop premises where the shop owner is likely to be around for a considerable period of time.

Under s 132, a seizure order is a lot more satisfactory especially when one is dealing with a temporary trading site such as a casual trading stall or indeed goods being sold out of the back of a van. Once the seizure order is made, the goods can be taken even if the infringer doesn't want them to be taken. This is a much better solution than the delivery up provision.

6.7.2.4 Seizure by copyright owner

Under pressure from copyright owners, s 133 of the Act was introduced and it allows copyright owners to seize infringing goods where it would not be possible for the owner to apply to the District Court. The owner or a representative of the owner can seize infringing copies, articles or protection defeating devices. This seizure can not be done at a person's permanent or regular place of business and force may not be used. Before the seizure the Gardaí must be notified of the time and place of the proposed seizure, and an exclusive licensee must also be notified.

If a person is aggrieved that goods have been seized from them, it is possible for the District Court to award damages to that person. This is a very unusual remedy and is one which could certainly be open to abuse. It remains to be seen how it is being practised on the ground. Presumably it will be used for, eg, outside rock concerts, etc, on a Saturday night, when a judge may not be easily available. Notwithstanding this, it is evident that risk may be attached to this procedure, especially if the copyright owner himself is not involved or solicitors are not involved and if security firms or other individuals are involved in these seizures.

6.8 Offences

A broad range of offences are provided for. There are four types of offences:

(a) offences in relation to infringing copies;
(b) offences in relation to articles used to make such copies;
(c) offences in relation to protection defeating devices;
(d) offences in relation to the performance of showing of work.

If a defendant shows that he was not aware that the work was an infringing copy, that the particular article was to be used or to make infringing copies or that the device was used to defeat rights protection measures, this is a defence. Therefore, if someone does any of the following with respect to an infringing copy that they know to be so, they are guilty of an offence:

(a) if they make for sale, rental or loan;
(b) if they sell, rent or lend or expose for sale, rental or loan;
(c) if they import into the state otherwise than for their private and domestic use;
(d) if in the course of business they have in their possession infringing copies;
(e) if they make copies available to the public to the extent that they prejudice the interest of the copyright owner.

As well as this if they do any of the acts (a)–(e) in respect of an article designed or adapted for making copies, or in respect of a protection defeating device, this is an offence also.

It is also an offence to perform in public a literary, dramatic or musical work, to play or show in public a sound recording or artist's work, original database or film or broadcast of work or include a work in a cable programme service without the permission of the rights owner. The penalties for any of these offences can, on indictment, include a fine not exceeding IR£1,500 and/or imprisonment not exceeding 12 months and on indictment, there is a possible fine not exceeding IR£100,000 and/or imprisonment not exceeding five years.

In criminal proceedings there is also a possibility for an order for delivery up, so that when a person is convicted of an offence or being satisfied that there is a *prima facie* case to answer, the court may order the delivery up of the particular articles.

Orders such as this will be made more frequently before a trial, as such orders would have the effect of preserving evidence.

6.9   Search warrants and seizure

Section 143 of the 2000 Act provides that when a District Court judge is satisfied that an offence is being committed or is about to be committed on a premises or at any place he may issue a warrant. It can also be issued where the District Court judge is satisfied by information on oath that evidence in respect of an offence can be found at any premises. The warrant granted is very broad in that it not only allows the Gardaí to enter the premises but also allows other persons nominated by the Gardaí (such as representatives of the copyright owners) to enter. The Gardaí can use reasonable force to seize the items and anyone on the premises can be required to give a name and address and anyone who obstructs or interferes with the person acting with the authority of a warrant is guilty of an offence.

CHAPTER 7

PROTECTION OF DATABASES AND COMPUTER PROGRAMS

Rosaleen Byrne

The purpose of this chapter is to explain the provisions of copyright law, and, in particular, those set out in the Copyright and Related Rights Act 2000 relating to computer programs and databases. This chapter will also outline the background to these legislative provisions with a view to providing students with a better understanding of the current legislative regime. Throughout this chapter, some of the matters which arise in practice in relation to these issues will be addressed.

7.1 Protection of computer programs

7.1.1 Background

To understand the current law and its application to computer programs, it is necessary to stop for a moment to consider the nature of a computer program. It is the nature of a computer program which has caused difficulties in relation to its legal protection. When the issue of protection of computer programs first arose, it was unclear whether or not they should be protected as literary works, artistic works, or indeed protected not by copyright but by some other legal right or simply through contractual provisions.

A computer program consists of a set of instructions, in electronic form, given to the central processing unit (CPU) of a computer to ensure that the computer performs certain functions. These instructions are not in human readable form. In general, however, when developing a computer program, developers set out the instructions that need to be given to the computer in language which is intelligible to a computer programmer. This is often supplemented by diagrams or flowcharts. The language, text and drawings, which are referred to as 'source code', are the result of skill and labour in creating the technical means by which instructions will be given to the CPU of a computer in the form of a program. In this form the computer program communicates information to human persons (albeit to reasonably skilled programmers only). Furthermore, in this form, there is a written expression of the computer program.

When these instructions are given to a computer, the instructions take the form of languages, known as 'machine code' or 'object code', which the computer will understand. Object code is a set of electronic pulses which communicates with the computer and is not expressed in a written form.

The background to the difficulty in relation to protecting computer programs is that, while the source code can be considered to be a literary or artistic work and can therefore be protected by copyright, there is no obvious category of copyright works into which the object code would fit.

The difficulty that presented itself to legislators and courts was the fact that although there was no obvious method for protecting the object code, if the object code was copied or reverse engineered the person who carried out the copying could have the benefit of the computer program, notwithstanding that they obtained that benefit as a result of the skill and labour of the author of the original source code underlying the object code in question. In the absence of any protection for source code and object code, the fruits of the skill and labour of the computer programmer could be exploited without any infringement having taken place. It was this concern that caused legislators to address the issue of protection of computer programs.

When this issue was initially considered, the World Intellectual Property Organisation (WIPO) suggested that computer programs should be protected by way of a new separate category or a *sui generis* right. Subsequently, however, mainly as a result of developments in the US (the Computer Software Copyright Act 1980), the international community, including the European Commission, decided to protect computer programs by categorising them as literary works so that they could avail of copyright protection.

7.1.2 International treaty law

Article 10(1) of the World Trade Organisation Agreement on Trade Related Aspects of Intellectual Property Rights (TRIPS) obliges Member States of the World Trade Organisation to protect computer programs as literary works under the Berne Convention.

Furthermore, the WIPO Copyright Treaty (agreed in Geneva in December 1996) clearly states that computer programs should be protected as literary works. Article 4 of the Treaty states as follows:

> Computer programs are protected as literary works within the meaning of Article 2 of the Berne Convention. Such protection applies to computer programs whatever may be the mode or form of their expression.

7.1.3 Developments at EU level

The European Commission published its Green Paper on *Copyright and the Challenge of Technology – Copyright Issues Requiring Immediate Action* in 1988.

This Green Paper was mainly concerned with the threat presented by digital copying and the competitive disadvantage of European producers of copyright goods as a result of differences in intellectual property laws in Member States. In response to submissions to this Green Paper the European Commission published a proposal for a Council Directive on the legal protection of computer programs. This proposal for a Directive resulted in intense debate in relation to issues such as the originality standard which should be applied to computer programs, the decompilation and reverse engineering of programs and the interoperability of computer programs. This Directive was adopted in 1991 and is referred to as the Software Directive (Council Directive 91/250/EEC, 14 May 1991, on the legal protection of computer programs).

7.1.4 Implementation of the Software Directive in Ireland

As we have already learned in Chapter 5, the Software Directive was initially implemented in Ireland by way of statutory instrument (SI 1993/26). This statutory instrument has been restated in the Copyright and Related Rights Act 2000.

As computer programs fall within the definition of 'literary works' a number of provisions relate to computer programs. Students should note, however, that ss 80–82 relate specifically to computer programs. These sections are included in Chapter 6 of the Act, under the heading 'Acts permitted in relation to works protected by copyright'. In other words, although the general provisions relating to the protection of literary works are applicable to computer programs, there are specific provisions regarding computer programs set out in the section of the Act dealing with exceptions to infringement of copyright.

7.1.5 Definition of 'computer program'

Section 2(1) of the Copyright and Related Rights Act 2000 provides that 'computer program' means a program which is original in the sense that it is the author's own intellectual creation and includes any design materials used for the preparation of the program. The Directive did not in fact contain any definition of a computer program; rather, it outlined some material that should be regarded as being within the definition and it also made reference to the relevant originality standard.

In addition, in keeping with the provisions of the Software Directive, we know from our introduction to the Act that literary work is defined in Section 2 of the Act as including a computer program.

7.1.6 Protection

Section 17(2) of the Act states that copyright subsists in original literary works. Having regard to the definitions outlined above, it is this section which confers copyright protection on computer programs.

Given the definition of computer programs in s 2(1) of the Act as an original program which is the author's own intellectual creation, it is arguable that the originality test for literary works which is generally considered to be a very low test (it simply means the work must not be copied) is somewhat raised in relation to computer programs. This is something which was required by Art 1(3) of the Software Directive which states that the work must be the author's own intellectual creation. The requirement to have a uniform level of originality for the granting of copyright protection throughout the European Union caused considerable difficulty when the Software Directive was being considered.

Section 17(3) of the Act, which states that copyright protection shall not extend to the ideas and principles which underlie any element of a work, is particularly important in the context of computer programs. Although the idea or expression dichotomy is a general principle of copyright law, this distinction was specifically required by Art 1(2) of the Software Directive.

7.1.7 Authorship and ownership

The provisions of ss 21–23 of the Copyright and Related Rights Act 2000 deal with authorship and ownership. These provisions also apply to computer programs.

In practice, one issue which is regularly encountered is the ownership of software which has been developed by a software developer or a specialised firm of software developers on behalf of a party who intends using the software in their business. In such a case, the general rule that the author of the work is the first owner of the copyright applies. Where software is developed by employees of the software development firm, then the rule that the employer owns the copyright in the software will apply. However, this will not change the position vis à vis the party who has commissioned the software to be developed as in either case the party who has commissioned the work will not be the owner of the copyright in the resulting software (unless, of course, this is agreed in writing).

It is also very common in the software industry for developers to work on a contract basis for software firms. In such cases, it is critical to recall that the rule relating to employees and employers will not apply and a specific clause in the contract of the independent contractor relating to ownership of intellectual property rights will be necessary. In most cases, a contract between the person hiring the contractor and the contractor will state that any intellectual property created by the contractor in the course of his work under the contract in question will be owned by the person who has contracted his services.

Whether acting for a software company in entering into a licence agreement (in the context of reviewing what warranties can be given in relation to ownership) or whether carrying out a due diligence exercise on behalf of a client intending to purchase a company whose main assets are intellectual property based, it is essential to enquire as to which parties were involved in the creation of the intellectual property work(s) in question. This applies to all classes of intellectual property work. However, it is particularly relevant in the case of software development, as one regularly finds that a number of parties of varying status might have worked together on a software development project and this could create complications in respect of authorship and as a result ownership of the software in question.

On a related note, regarding employees, the 2000 Act states that if a work is created by an employee in the course of his employment by his employer then copyright in the work will be owned by the employer unless there is an agreement in writing to the contrary. It is important, therefore, to check all employment contracts and other agreements which may exist between employee and employer to see whether anything has been agreed to the contrary in writing.

In practice, companies regularly pay software developers to develop software on their behalf without first having agreed that the company who has commissioned the work should own the copyright in the work. Cases where this happens range from the development of websites to the development of a company's core software. Generally, your clients will assume that once they have paid for something they own it. This is not the case unless specifically agreed in writing.

Some more sophisticated clients will be more alive to the issue of IP ownership and in the event that they engage lawyers to draft or finalise large software development contracts, ownership of intellectual property rights is usually the most contentious issue and the one that takes the longest to negotiate.

In practice, it is common for a software developer to retain ownership of the copyright in the core computer program which they develop and they license this to their client on a non-exclusive basis. By licensing on a non-exclusive basis, this leaves the software developer free to license its core software to other parties. In the event that a party had contracted a software developer to develop specific bespoke software for their specific needs, then the copyright in this bespoke software would usually be assigned to the client or the client would be given a sole or exclusive licence in respect of same. In certain cases, where the software to be developed is of a specialised and specific nature, the software developer might have no difficulty in assigning the copyright in it to the third party who has commissioned it, as it may have no commercial value as regards licensing it to other parties.

In cases where parties to a software development contract fail to address the issue of copyright ownership in advance of the completion of the project and the party who has commissioned the work pays a fee for the development work, it may be possible, if acting for this party, to rely on equitable concepts such as implied contract and constructive trusts in relation to the ownership of copyright in any resulting computer program. Essentially, the person who commissioned the computer program could argue that although, based on s 23 of the Act, the author is the legal owner of the copyright, the party who commissioned and paid for the work at the very least would have an implied licence to use the work and may in fact be the beneficial owner of same. See *John Richardson Computers Ltd v Flanders* [1993] FSR 497. See also *Pasterfield v Denham and Another* [1999] FSR 169.

7.1.8 Restricted acts

Section 37(1) of the Copyright and Related Rights Act 2000 sets out the acts which are restricted by copyright in a work, ie, the acts which the right holder has the exclusive right to do or to authorise others to do. These acts are as follows:

(a) to copy the work;
(b) to make the work available to the public;
(c) to make an adaptation of the work or to undertake any of the acts referred to in (a) or (b) in relation to an adaptation.

These rights are addressed in further detail in:

(a) s 39 – the reproduction right;
(b) s 40 – the making available right;
(c) s 41 – the distribution right;
(d) s 42 – the rental and lending right;
(e) s 43 – adaptations.

Section 37(2) makes it clear that copyright in a work is infringed by a person who, without the licence of the copyright owner, undertakes or authorises another to undertake any of the restricted acts.

7.1.8.1 The reproduction right

In relation to the right to restrict the copying of a work it is necessary to take account of s 39(1)(a) of the Act. This section states that copying includes storing the work in any medium and making copies of the work which are transient or incidental to some other use of the work. Given this very broad definition of the term 'copying' almost any use of a computer program will constitute copying. Therefore even if a backup copy of a computer program is made or a computer program is incidentally cached on the hard drive of a computer without the knowledge of the computer user this will constitute copying. In the event that this is done without the licence or authorisation of the copyright owner this will constitute an infringement. Thankfully, however, there are other provisions of the legislation which set out exceptions to this very broad definition (see ss 80, 82 and 87 of the Act) and which will be considered later in this chapter.

7.1.8.2 Distribution of computer programs

The right to make available to the public the copies of a work is commonly known as the 'making available right'. This right is set out in s 40 of the Act and it applies *inter alia* to literary works (including computer programs). This section would apply where the copyright owner of a computer program distributes the program over the internet. The distribution of tangible copies of computer programs is covered by the distribution right in s 41 of the Act.

7.1.8.3 Making an adaptation

The making of an adaptation of a work is also a restricted act. Section 43(2) of the Act states that in relation to a computer program, adaptation includes the translation, arrangement or other alteration of the computer program and in particular it includes the making of a version of the computer program in which it is converted into or out of a computer language or code or into a different computer language or code.

7.1.9 Exceptions to restricted acts

Given the very broad scope of acts which are defined as restricted acts, almost any use of a computer program could amount to a restricted act. It is for this reason that it was necessary to provide a set of exceptions to the restricted acts which are specific to computer programs. These exceptions are as follows:

7.1.9.1 Backup copies

Section 80 of the 2000 Act states that it is not an infringement of the copyright in a computer program for a lawful (ie, a party who is licensed by or on behalf of the copyright owner) user of a computer program to make a backup copy of it, which is necessary for him to have for the purpose of his lawful use. This exception relating to the making of backup copies is clearly linked to the scope of the licence which the lawful user has as it specifically refers to backup copies necessary for the purpose of his lawful use. Section 80(2) states that the person is a 'lawful user' of a computer program where he has a right to use the program to undertake any act restricted by copyright.

7.1.9.2 Decompilation right

Section 81(1) of the Act states that it is not an infringement of the copyright in the computer program for a lawful user to make a copy, a translation, adaptation, arrangement or any other alteration to the computer program in order to achieve interoperability with that program of an independently created computer program. This provision, which is based on Art 6 of the Software Directive, is intended to allow reverse engineering of a computer program created or written by a right holder in order to produce an interoperable program. This exception is subject to three conditions being complied with. These are as follows:

(a) the acts are performed by the lawful user or on his behalf by a person authorised to do so;

(b) the information necessary to achieve interoperability has not previously been available to the person who carries out the acts; and

(c) the permitted acts are confined to the parts of the original program which are necessary to achieve interoperability.

Section 81(2) goes on to say that s 81(1) does not permit the information obtained through its application to be used other than to achieve interoperability of an independently created computer program, and it also expressly states that it does not permit the information obtained to be used for the development, production or marketing of a computer program substantially similar in its expression, or for any other act which infringes copyright.

    The reason this exception is necessary is that computer programs do not work in isolation. They perform their primary function along with other hardware and software and they generally interact with other hardware and software in giving instructions to a computer. If programs could not be modified so as to allow them to interact with other programs and hardware, their usefulness would be greatly hampered. Interoperability is the ability of one computer program to communicate with another. This section permits the program to be decompiled, that is, to be converted from object code to source code, in the specific circumstances to which the exception applies.

7.1.9.3 Incidental acts

Section 82 of the Act states that it is not an infringement of the copyright in a computer program for a lawful user to make a copy of a whole or part of the program or to translate, adapt or arrange the program where such actions are necessary for the use of the program by the lawful user in accordance with its intended use. The purpose of this section is to ensure that the lawful user is entitled to carry out certain activities related to the work and in particular that the technical copying, translation and adaptation, which may occur incidentally in the use of the computer program, do not constitute an infringement.

Section 82(2) states that it is not an infringement of the copyright in the computer program for a lawful user to observe, test or study the functioning of the program in order to determine the ideas and principles which lie behind any element of the program provided that he does so while performing the acts of loading, displaying, running, transmitting or storing the program which he is authorised to do.

Section 87 of the Act limits the very broad definition of copying set out in s 39 of the Act. Section 87 is directed at ensuring that transient and incidental copies which are technically required for the viewing of or listening to the work by a person to whom the work has been made lawfully available (ie, a lawful user) does not constitute an infringement. This is directed at ensuring, for example, that the caching of a computer program or the caching of a literary work in electronic form on the hard drive of a computer does not constitute an infringement of copyright.

7.2 Protection of databases

In considering the legal issues arising in the context of the protection of databases, it is necessary to distinguish between original databases, which can avail of copyright protection, and databases which represent the creation of a mechanical collection or arrangement of facts or information and in which there has been no exercise of skill or judgment. The latter form of database, while not qualifying for copyright protection, can be protected by a new right which was introduced in the 2000 Act, known as the database right.

This database right is a *sui generis* right relating specifically to databases. Part V of the Act which deals with the database right implements this *sui generis* right which was first introduced by Council Directive 96/9/EC on the legal protection of databases (Database Directive). The purpose of that Directive was to ensure uniform protection for databases throughout Member States.

7.2.1 Original databases

'Original database' is defined in s 2 of the Copyright and Related Rights Act 2000 as being:

> A database in any form which by reason of the selection or arrangement of its contents constitutes the original intellectual creation of the author.

It is this ingredient of 'original intellectual creation' which entitles an original database to protection by way of copyright.

When considering whether or not there is sufficient judgment and skill exercised in creating a database so as to satisfy this test of original intellectual creation, readers should bear in mind that whether or not copyright subsists in the contents of the database is irrelevant. Section 17(3) of the Act states that copyright protection shall, in respect of original databases, not extend to their contents and is without prejudice to any rights subsisting in those contents.

Databases which usually qualify for copyright protection are databases which are in the nature of compilations. By way of example, in the case of *Football League Ltd v Littlewood Pools Ltd* [1950] Ch 637 Upjohn J considered that considerable skill and judgment was applied. In this case, the issue was whether or not a compilation, which consisted of a list of football fixtures, constituted a literary work. Many of the cases relating to compilations of works and whether or not they constitute literary works deal with issues that are relevant to ascertaining whether a database constitutes an original database and therefore qualifies for copyright protection. Readers should note that many of the cases where it has been considered that the element of skill, labour and judgment has been missing have involved a compilation of works from pre-existing sources and works relating to factual issues, such as the publication of railway timetables.

If a database can satisfy the test of the author's original intellectual creation, then it can benefit from copyright protection and it is protected for a period of the life of the author plus 70 years.

7.2.2 'Non-original' databases

Part V of the Act deals with database rights. Where a database does not qualify as an original database then a lesser form of protection is provided for such 'non-original' databases. Non-original databases are referred to in the Act simply as 'databases'.

A database is defined in s 2 of the Act as being:

> ... a collection of independent works, data or other materials, arranged in a systematic or methodical way and individually accessible by any means but excludes computer programs used in the making or operation of a database.

The Database Directive contains a similar definition and in commenting on this part of the Directive, Laddie J has stated:

> ... to be independent, the works, data, or other materials should be capable of being, or intended to be appreciated or useful in isolation. This would not include individual chapters in a literary work or scenes in a dramatic work.

7.2.3 Qualifying for protection

The database right covers electronic and non-electronic arrangements and in order to qualify for database protection the works must be systematically or methodically organised. By way of example, arrangement of the works in an alphabetic or chronological manner would be sufficient to satisfy this requirement.

In addition to the requirement that the work must be systematically or methodically organised, in order to qualify for protection substantial investment must have been made in the creation of the database. Section 321 provides that where substantial investment has been incurred in obtaining, verifying, or presenting the contents of the database then the *sui generis* right shall exist. Investment of resources as referred to in the Act means 'financial, human or technical resources' and the reference to substantial means 'quantity or quality or a combination of both'.

Where a copyright work is included in a database, copyright shall continue to subsist in that work as well as a separate database right subsisting in the database. It is not material whether the database or its contents are capable of being protected by copyright, as the purpose of the database right is to protect the investment and the effort which has been undertaken to create the database.

7.2.4 Acts restricted by the database rights

The owner of a database right has the right to undertake or to authorise others to undertake the following acts in relation to all or a substantial part of the contents of the database:

(a) extraction;

(b) re-utilisation.

The database right is infringed by a person who without the licence of the owner of the database right undertakes or authorises another to undertake either of these restricted acts.

Extraction is defined in s 320(1) of the Act in the same terms as in the Database Directive as:

> The permanent or temporary transfer of all or a substantial part of the contents to another medium by any means or any form.

Re-utilisation is defined in s 320(1) of the Act as:

> ... in relation to the contents of a database making those contents available to the public by any means.

Although there is no definition of 'substantial' in the Act, s 324(3) states that for the purposes of this part of the Act, the repeated and systematic extraction or re-utilisation of insubstantial parts of the contents of a database which conflicts with the normal exploitation of a database or which prejudices the interests of the maker of the database shall be deemed to be extraction or re-utilisation of a substantial part of the contents.

In other words, a one-off action by itself in relation to an insubstantial part of the database will not constitute an infringement of the database right. However, if carried out repeatedly, it will be contrary to s 324 and will constitute an infringement.

7.2.5 Term of protection of database right

The database right expires 15 years from the end of the calendar year in which the making of the database was completed.

However, any substantial change to the contents of the database, including a substantial change resulting from the accumulation of successive additions, deletions or alterations which would result in the database being considered to be a substantial new investment, shall qualify the database resulting from that investment for its own terms of protection. Accordingly, a database which is continually updated could have the benefit of protection under this new database right indefinitely.

To date, there has only been one significant case relating to the interpretation of the Database Directive. This case is *British Horseracing Board Ltd and Others v William Hill Organisation Ltd* [2001] 2 CMLR 12. Judgment in this matter was given by Mr Justice Laddie on 9 February 2001. This case was concerned with the extent to which the plaintiffs could prevent the defendant from using, without their licence, certain data which according to the plaintiff had been derived indirectly from them.

In this case, it was argued, that the indirect capture of data (ie, through a third party) from a database was not an extraction as it merely replicated the data. This argument was rejected. It was also argued that in the case of the database that was consistently updated, repeated and systematic taking of minor data could not be considered to be cumulative and therefore could not be considered to be an infringement, as the data was taken from different databases. This argument was also rejected. The case has been appealed and the Court of Appeal has referred a number of questions to the ECJ.

7.3 Summary

Hopefully the information given in this chapter will be sufficient to equip students when advising in relation to the protection of computer programs and databases. In considering any issues which arise in practice in relation to these two forms of work, the most important points to address are the following:

- What form of protection is available for the work in question?
- What is the duration of the protection afforded?
- Are all aspects of the work protected?
- Who created the work?
- Who owns the rights in the work?
- Apart from copyright or database right protection, could any other forms of intellectual property protect the work?
- How best should the work be exploited?
- In considering whether an infringement has taken place, consider what are the restricted acts which are applicable to each type of work?
- In the case of infringement, do any of the exemptions apply?

CHAPTER 8

INDUSTRIAL DESIGNS

Garrett Breen

8.1 Introduction

The law relating to industrial designs in Ireland has recently been in a state of change. Decades ago, most intellectual property in Ireland was dealt with in the Industrial and Commercial Property (Protection) Act 1927. This Act was largely repealed, apart from those sections dealing with industrial designs. However, this remaining legislation relating to industrial designs in Ireland has recently been replaced by the Industrial Designs Act 2001 (the 2001 Act), which repeals the 1927 Act.

In order to try and understand what an industrial design is, it is important to go back to the definition contained in the 1927 Act. In that Act, 'design' was defined as follows:

(a) only the features of shape, configuration, pattern or ornament;
(b) applied to any article;
(c) by any industrial process or means;
(d) whether manual, mechanical or chemical;
(e) separate or combined, which in the finished article;
(f) appeal to and are judged solely by the eye;
(g) but does not include any mode or principal of construction or anything which is in substance a mere mechanical device.

Essentially, an industrial design under the 1927 Act meant those parts of an article which are totally non-functional in nature but which make it look nice and seem appealing to a viewer or consumer. Those features of a product which make it look trendy, pretty and generally appealing to the eye are the features of the 'industrial design' of that product. They do not increase the functionality of the product; they merely make it look better.

A china cup may have detailed ornamentation and a nice shape, but these features do nothing except make the cup look better and more attractive. They do not make the cup any easier to drink out of. A football jersey or a dress need only have plain material front and back with appropriate places for the arms, head, etc. However, most dresses and football jerseys have patterned material, logos and different features, such as short sleeves, flares, frills, etc. All of these features do nothing to improve the function of the item. However, they do make the item more appealing to the eye, more fashionable and more up-to-date. They comprise the industrial design of the product.

Going back to the 1927 definition, it is clear that these design features which are non-functional need to be applied to the article by some kind of industrial process such as by painting, sand blasting, dipping, etc.

8.2 Definition of design

The definition of a design in the 2001 Act differs in some respects from the definition in the 1927 Act. In the 2001 Act, it states that a design means the appearance of the whole or a part of a product resulting from the features of, in particular:

- the lines;
- contours;
- colour;
- shape;
- texture or materials of the product itself;
- its ornamentation.

A product is defined as any:

- industrial or handicraft item;
- including parts intended to be assembled into a complex product;
- packaging get up, graphics, symbols and typographical type faces;
- but not including computer programmes.

The difference in the definitions between the 1927 Act and the 2001 Act are as follows:

(a) There is no longer a requirement for the design to *solely* have eye appeal as it is the appearance of the whole or a part of a product which is the design.

(b) There is now a requirement that the design should be novel on a worldwide basis and not just within the Irish jurisdiction. Under the old law, the novelty requirement was confined to publication within the Irish jurisdiction. However, in the 2001 Act, where a designer tests the market in the 12-month period preceding the filing for registration, the design will not be deemed to have lost novelty.

(c) Functional designs are excluded as under the old Act. However, the exclusion in the new Act refers to it being solely functional, which is a narrow definition. In other words, if it has one functional aspect, it is not necessarily disqualified. Under s 16(2) of the new Act, new products which are designed in a particular way so that they interconnect or fit into another product with the purpose of performing a function do not have registrable rights.

8.3 Protection of industrial designs

Industrial designs are registerable intellectual property rights. In Ireland, government policy as per the 2001 Act is that there should always be a system of registration of industrial designs. If a design comes within the definition of an industrial design, then it really needs to be registered in order for it to be protected.

In the 1927 Act, if your design was registerable (ie, came within the definition of an industrial design) but you had not registered such a design, copyright did not subsist in the design and nothing could be done to stop infringers.

Under the new Act, s 87 (as inserted by s 31(a) of the Copyright and Related Rights Act 2000) provides for copyright in a registered design which expires 25 years after the filing date or the expiry of copyright, whichever is the sooner.

8.4 Community design right

Notwithstanding the fact that in Ireland we encourage registration of industrial designs, there are in force in Ireland at the moment European Regulations known as the Community Design Regulations (SI 2002/2942). They have been in force in Ireland since 6 March 2002. These Regulations provide a system for community-wide legal protection of designs. It has two elements, described below.

8.4.1 An unregistered community design right (UCD)

This confers an automatic short term protection against the copying of industrial designs. If one makes products incorporating the designs available to the public, the right comes into existence. This right only has a three-year duration and is limited only to the right to forbid others to use copies of the original designs.

In order for the UCD to come into existence it must be made available to the public within the European Union. This can be done in numerous ways, eg by putting the product on the market, by publishing the design in a magazine or by disclosing the design in an exhibition or on television. It is therefore not necessary that the physical product be put on the market in Europe but rather that people who would be aware of such products would have reasonably known about the new design.

The three-year protection starts on the date of the disclosure to the public. Therefore if you wish to have a European-wide protection it might be useful to disclose your design, decide within 12 months whether you wish to register the UCD and then go ahead and register under the registered community design right.

8.4.2 Registered community design right (RCD)

This is going to be similar to the community trade mark and will be administered by the Office for Harmonisation in the Internal Market (OHIM) in Alicante, Spain. An RCD may be protected for a maximum of 25 years. The initial term of protection is five years, with renewal for four consecutive five-year periods. It is expected that one may be able to apply for an RCD as and from March/April 2003.

Under the procedure it will be possible for the applicant to file a so-called 'multiple application'. This means that different applications of the same design can be combined in one single RCD application. The only limit is that the products fall within the scope of the same class of products as defined in the international classification for industrial design. For example, if an application is put in for design protection for a nice pattern on cups, you can also extend this application to cups, saucers or any other type of crockery within the particular class.

It is difficult for a company to assess whether a particular design will in fact be successful. To avoid the necessity for a company to register all its designs, the system offers the possibility (as mentioned above) of a period of grace of 12 months during which a design can be tested freely in the market without jeopardising the novelty of the design. In addition an applicant who wishes to keep its design secret in order to prepare a marketing strategy can ask for deferment of publication of the design for a period of 30 months.

It is important to remember that the rights that will come into existence by virtue of the Community Design Regulations will not be enforceable against uses of designs of components of complex products which must match the larger components, eg visible spare parts for vehicles for repair purposes.

8.5 What kind of design is registerable under the new 2001 Act?

Under s 11 of the Act, a design is registerable as long as it is *new* and has individual character. As mentioned above, it must have worldwide novelty and not just novelty in Ireland.

8.6 What does 'new' mean?

Under s 12, a design is new if no design is identical to it or has been previously made available to the public before the filing date for registration or if priority has been claimed to the date of priority. When a design is being applied for it will be deemed identical to another design when its features differ in immaterial details.

As mentioned above, a design is new where nothing like it has been previously made available to the public. A design is not deemed to have been made available to the public if it has been made available to third parties under conditions of confidentiality. This could be on occasions where an actual Confidentiality Agreement exists or where the circumstances surrounding the publication imply that an obligation of confidentiality existed between the parties. Where the design has been made available to the public without the consent of the author, this is not necessarily a 'making available' either.

8.7 Individual character

A design has individual character if the overall impression it produces on an informed user differs from the overall impression produced on an informed user by a design which has been available to the public before the filing date of the application for registration or, where priority was claimed, the date of priority.

In assessing the individual character of a design, the degree of freedom of the author of the design in developing it is taken into consideration. In other words, if the author of the design was not fettered in any way by any functional constraints or by instructions from a third party in relation to the way in which it should be designed then this will indicate, all the more, the fact that it is an industrial design.

8.8 Component parts

As regards component parts of a complex product, s 14 of the 2001 Act states that such a component part is only considered new and to have individual character if the component remains visible during normal use and where the component itself meets the novelty and individual character requirements. An example of this may be the wing mirrors of a car. This component part of the car is visible during normal use and may have a shape not related to the functionality of the wing mirror.

A design is not registerable if it conflicts with an earlier design right. This is no different to other registered intellectual property rights.

8.9 Designs dictated by technical functions and designs of interconnections

Section 16 of the 2001 Act sets out very specific provisions in relation to the registration of designs, which involve functionality. Section 16(1) states that the features of a product which are solely dictated by function are not registerable. This restates the definition of an industrial design. Under s 16(2) if a design is produced in its exact form or dimensions so that it can cause an overall product to function, this again is not registerable. This would apply to a spare part, which would be inserted into a complex machine.

However, there is an exemption to this under s 63 where it may be that an article, which in itself is composed of several parts or connections of parts, connects in order to produce the pleasing result. These shapes are registerable. They may not have any other function other than to be able to connect in a modular form; but they connect in such a way that they produce a result which is appealing to the eye. An example of this might be a flexible watch strap which, although very well-designed from a visual point of view, in fact consists of several moving parts which are linked to each other by virtue of their shape.

8.10 Ownership of a design

As with most intellectual property rights the creator of a design is the author. A design can be created using a computer although a computer program itself cannot be an industrial design. It is possible for an author to create an industrial design using a computer programme (CAD). The person who makes the arrangements necessary for the creation of a design is the author.

In situations where there is an employer/employee relationship, this is dealt with in s 19 of the 2001 Act. The owner is deemed to be the employer but the employee has an entitlement to be cited as the creator of the design on the register.

8.11 Filing date

The filing date of the application is the date on which the information and all fees are filed in the Patents Office. This is a very important date because it establishes the date at which matters such as novelty and individual character are decided, and, in particular, whether there has been a making available of the design to the public prior to this date. The filing date gives the proprietor of the design precedence over another application which may be filed at another date.

8.12 Priority right

This right, in s 26, gives a person who has filed an application in or in respect of a Paris Convention country or a member country of the World Trade Organisation (WTO) a right of priority for six months from the date of filing of the foreign application.

8.13 When does registration take effect?

The registration of a design takes effect from the date of application although it might take some time for an application to eventually get registered. When it does become registered, the registration dates back to the date of application.

8.14 What is a design right and what does it entitle the owner to do?

Under s 42 of the 2001 Act, a right is created which is known as the design right. The person recorded as the proprietor of the design shall be the design right owner. The design right gives registered proprietors the exclusive right to use the design and authorise others to use it including the right to:

(a) make;
(b) offer;
(c) put on the market;
(d) import or export;
(e) use the product;
(f) stock the product.

The design right lasts for a maximum period of 25 years in total, which consists of five-yearly renewable periods. Under the old 1927 Act, 15 years was the maximum period for protection.

If a design right lapses (because it has not been renewed), it is possible to apply to have it put back providing that you can show that you took reasonable care.

8.15 Compulsory licences

As with patents it is possible to obtain a compulsory licence of a design. The compulsory licence of a design can be granted if there is a demand for the product in the State and this is not being met in the State. Also if the demand for the design is being met by importing products from a country other than from a WTO country, then it is possible to request a compulsory licence.

8.16 Infringement

Under s 50 of the Copyright and Related Rights Act 2000, infringement of the design right occurs when one undertakes one of the acts, which is the exclusive right of the proprietor (mentioned at section 8.14 above).

An infringement does not take place by the reproduction of a feature of the design, which is not taken into account in determining whether the design is registerable or not.

8.17 Remedies

The remedies available to the design right holder are very similar to those available under the 2000 Act. The design holder can issue proceedings in the court for damages or an account of profits. If during the course of those proceedings the validity of a design right is called into question, the court may make a declaration that the design right is registerable and is properly registered. This is a very good shield against any further challenges to the design right.

8.18 Groundless threats

Under s 56 it is possible for a proposed defendant to bring proceedings against someone who is accusing that party of infringement on the basis that groundless threats of proceedings are being made. Remedies of injunction, a declaration that the threat was groundless and damages are available in these circumstances.

8.19 Rights of seizure and delivery up

As with the Copyright and Related Rights Act 2000, the proprietor of a design has the ability to apply for orders for seizure and delivery up of infringing designs. If a licensee is exploiting the designs, the exclusive licensee has the same rights as the design's proprietor in relation to infringement. If the licensee is a non-exclusive licensee, that licensee could call upon the proprietor to act.

8.20 Offences

It is an offence to do any of the following in relation to design while a design right is in force:

(a) use the design otherwise for private and domestic use;
(b) make the design for sale or rent;
(c) sell or rent or offer or expose for sale or rent the design;
(d) import the design into the state otherwise than for private or domestic use;
(e) export the design or have the copies of the design in custody or control in the course of a business.

In addition to the above a person who makes, sells, rents or offers to expose for sale or rent, imports into the state or has in his possession custody or control an article designed to make an infringing copy of the design is guilty of an offence.

Such a person is liable in summary conviction to a fine not exceeding €1905 or 12 months' imprisonment or both, or a conviction or indictment of €127,000 or imprisonment for a term not exceeding five years.

8.21 Falsification of register

It is also an offence to make or cause to be made forced entry into the register or to claim in writing or otherwise something to be a copy or reproduction of entry in the register when it is not.

8.22 Conclusion

Industrial design law in Ireland now that it has been updated will probably encourage new registration. The new system recognises the needs of the business community in a more practical way.

"Yours to use, but not to copy"

Photocopying this work is illegal under the Copyright Acts. Theft of intellectual property is just as illegal as theft of physical property, and anyone so doing will be subject to legal action.

CHAPTER 9

INTELLECTUAL PROPERTY LICENCES

Tara MacMahon

9.1 Introduction

What is an intellectual property (IP) licence? A licence is a permission to do something that is otherwise prohibited. An IP licence permits the licensee to use the IP in question on certain conditions, in a manner which would, but for the licence, infringe the rights of the IP owner.

IP licences take many forms. For example, a franchise agreement will include, as part of its terms, a licence to the franchisee to use the franchisor's trade marks and know-how in the course of carrying on the franchised business. Similarly, a sub-contract manufacturing agreement will include, as part of its terms, a licence to the sub-contractor to use the contracting party's IP for the purposes of manufacturing the products.

In certain circumstances, it is possible for a licence of IP to be implied, by virtue of the actions and/or intentions of the parties. However, it is always advisable for a licence of IP to be documented in writing. A written licence agreement is the only way to prevent, as far as possible, any dispute between the parties, at a later stage, as to the terms on which the licensee is permitted to use the licensed IP, and the rights and obligations of the licensor and licensee attaching to the licence.

9.1.1 Legislative framework

Sections 32–36 of the Trade Marks Act 1996 deal specifically with licences of registered trade marks, although other provisions of that Act are also relevant to the licensing of registered trade marks. See, for example, s 29, which deals with registerable transactions. Section 32 specifically states that a licence of a registered trade mark will not be effective unless it is in writing and signed by or on behalf of the grantor (s 32(3)).

Sections 68–75 of the Patents Act 1992 deal specifically with the licensing of patents. Primarily, these sections deal with compulsory licences, and applications for licences of right. Again, other provisions of that Act are also relevant to the licensing of patents. In particular, s 83 renders null and void (subject to limited exceptions) certain restrictive conditions in contracts relating to the licence of patents. These are:

(a) any prohibition or restriction on the use of any product or process which was supplied by or owned by a party who is not a party to the contract or a nominee of a party to the contract (s 83(1)(a));

(b) any requirement to acquire from the other party to the contract or his nominee, any product which is not the subject of a patent application or granted patent (s 83(1)(b)).

The Patents Act does not specifically provide that a patent licence must be in writing in order to be effective. However, it is always advisable for a patent licence to be in writing.

Sections 120–22, 135 and 136 of the Copyright and Related Rights Act 2000 deal with the licensing of copyright and database rights (s 338), but again, other provisions of this

Act are also relevant to the licensing of these rights. The Act does not state that all licences of copyright must be in writing. It does, however, provide that exclusive licences of copyright must be in writing in order to benefit from the provisions relating to exclusive licences under this Act (s 122(1)).

9.2 Recordal of licences

The licence of a registered trade mark is a registerable transaction under the Trade Marks Act 1996 (s 29(2)(b)) and places a statutory obligation to record the licence at the Trade Marks Registry. Failure to record the licence at the Irish Trade Marks Registry results in a number of disadvantages, particularly to the licensee, in particular:

(a) the licence is ineffective as against any person acquiring a conflicting interest in or under the registered trade mark in ignorance of the licence (s 29(3)(a));

(b) the licensee will not be entitled to benefit from the provisions of s 34 or s 35 of the Act (s 29(3)(b)) (ss 34 and 35 grant certain rights to licensees in the event that a third party is infringing the licensed registered trade mark, eg, the right to take infringement proceedings in its own name);

(c) the licensee will be unable to recover damages or an account of profits in respect of any infringement of the registered trade mark (s 29(4)).

The Patents Act 1992 places a statutory obligation to record any licences granted in respect of a patent or a published patent application at the Patents Office (s 85(1)). The penalty for non-recordal is that a document in respect of which there has been no recordal will only be admitted in any court as evidence of title if the court so directs (s 85(7)). The Patents Act does not specify any time scale within which this recordal must be made.

As copyright is an unregistered right, there is no registry at which a copyright licence can be recorded.

9.3 Competition law issues

Article 81 of the Treaty of Rome prohibits agreements which have as their object or effect the prevention, restriction or distortion of competition, and which may affect trade between Member States. Under Irish law, s 4 of the Competition Act 2002 prohibits agreements which prevent, restrict or distort competition in the state. As a result, any provision in an IP licence agreement which prevents, restricts or distorts competition (or is intended to do so) may be void and unenforceable. In serious cases, the European Commission may also impose fines on undertakings for breach of Art 81(1). In Ireland, the Competition Authority has the power to take a court action for breach of s 4 or Art 81 which may result in the imposition of fines by an Irish court. In addition, persons adversely affected by a prohibited agreement (including third parties) may take an action in the Irish courts for breach of s 4. Finally, breach of s 4 or Art 81 is a criminal offence in Irish law.

However, the competition authorities accept that the inclusion of restrictive provisions (such as exclusivity) in licence agreements are often necessary in order to meet the commercial requirements of the parties. In view of this, the European Commission has issued two block exemptions which are of particular relevance to IP licence agreements.

The most important of these is the Technology Transfer Block Exemption (TTBE) (Council Regulation EC/240/96). This applies to pure patent licences, pure know-how licences and mixed patent and know-how licences, and to other IP if ancillary to the patent and know-how licence. Although it does not apply to licences relating primarily to design, copyright or trade marks, when drafting licences of design, copyright or trade marks, reference should be made to the TTBE for guidance as to whether the licence falls within any competition law constraints. It should be noted that the TTBE is currently under review. In December 2001 the European Commission adopted a Report (Commission Evaluation Report on the Transfer of Technology Block Exemption No 240/96: Technology Transfer Agreement under Art 81), which made a preliminary assessment of the TTBE, put forward preliminary policy proposals for reform, and invited comments on a series of issues.

The other block exemption is the more recent Vertical Agreements Block Exemption (Council Regulation EC/2790/99). This applies to agreements concerned with the supply of products between parties operating at different levels of trade, which can include retail franchise agreements and other arrangements where a licence of trade marks or other IP rights forms an element (but not the primary object) of the arrangement.

In order to ensure compliance with competition law, it is important to ensure that, when drafting an IP licence agreement, the agreement does not contravene either the Vertical Agreements Block Exemption or the TTBE. As the Vertical Agreements exemption is of limited application to IP licensing, this chapter focuses on the TTBE. In this chapter reference is made to some of the provisions of the TTBE, where they are relevant to the issues being discussed. However, the TTBE contains a number of other provisions which are not outlined in this chapter, and therefore, when drafting any IP licence agreement, reference should be made at all times to the entire text of the TTBE.

9.4   Pre-contract considerations

As with any commercial agreement it is advisable that, before entering into an IP licence agreement, both the licensor and the licensee carry out certain investigations in respect of the other party, and the subject matter of the agreement.

A licensee will be primarily concerned with investigating the IP which is to be licensed to it. For example, where the licensed IP comprises registered IP (eg, patents, trade marks, registered designs), the licensee may wish to carry out its own independent searches to satisfy itself as to the status of these registrations. Although the licensee will also seek warranties in respect of these issues, a warranty only offers limited comfort. Ascertaining the true position as to the status of the registered IP is the only way a licensee can properly estimate the value of the licence which is to be granted to it.

A licensor will be primarily concerned with investigating the licensee, eg, whether it is financially sound, whether it will be in a position to pay the royalties and whether it has the facilities to properly manufacture, market and sell the products utilising or incorporating the licensed IP.

9.5   Anatomy of a licence agreement

As a starting point, it should be noted that, as with all contracts, general contractual principles (eg, offer, acceptance, consideration, etc) apply to licence agreements.

The provisions of a licence agreement will very much depend on the nature of the IP which is being licensed, ie, whether it comprises patents, trade marks, confidential know-how, copyright, database rights, etc.

Having said this, the key provisions of an IP licence agreement are outlined below. Some of these provisions are of greater importance to the licensee, whilst others are of greater importance to the licensor. It is equally important to both parties, however, that the agreement is clear and unambiguous, and outlines all issues relevant to the commercial arrangement between the parties.

The key provisions of an IP licence agreement are:

(a) identity of the parties;
(b) description of the licensed IP;
(c) scope of the licence – namely, permitted purpose, exclusivity, territory, right to sub-contract, right to sub-licence;
(d) assignability;
(e) term of the licence and renewal provisions;
(f) termination provisions;
(g) consideration or payment provisions;
(h) ownership of improvements;
(i) warranties;
(j) indemnities;
(k) infringement claims against third parties;
(l) confidentiality;
(m) obligations of licensor;
(n) obligations of licensee;
(o) governing law, jurisdiction, dispute resolution.

9.5.1 Identity of the parties to the agreement

The agreement should identify the correct legal entities which are to be licensed under the agreement. For example, is the licensee executing the agreement on behalf of all its subsidiaries, or only on behalf of itself? (If an agreement is being executed on behalf of all subsidiaries of a licensee, this could give rise to privity of contract issues.)

9.5.2 Description of the licensed IP

The agreement should clearly and comprehensively identify the IP which is the subject matter of the licence agreement. This is critical, as failure to do so could mean that the licensor is licensing more IP than it intended, or that the licensee is not granted the right to use all IP which it requires.

Where the licensed IP comprises any registered IP, or applications for registered IP, full details of these applications and registrations should be provided in a schedule to the agreement. Where the licensed IP comprises any granted patents or patent applications, the agreement should make it clear that the licence includes a licence of all renewals, reissues and extensions of such granted patents and patent applications.

Where the licensed IP comprises unregistered IP (eg, copyright, unregistered marks, database rights, know-how), the exercise of identifying the IP which is to be the subject matter of the agreement is more difficult. Usually, this is defined by reference to a particular product or process (eg, 'all IP required for the manufacture of [...]' or 'all IP comprised in the product currently known as [...]').

9.5.3 The scope of the permitted purpose

The agreement should make clear the purpose for which the licensee is permitted to use the licensed IP. For example, is the licensee permitted to use the licensed IP for the purposes of research and development? For the manufacture of any product or only specified products? For marketing and sale of the products? For use in any process/only specified processes?

The specific acts that are to be permitted depend on the nature of the licensed IP, and the manner in which it can be infringed.

A registered trade mark, for example, can be licensed for any use in relation to the products or services for which it is registered, where such use, if carried out without consent, would constitute registered trade mark infringement. This licence can be conferred in general terms, or in relation to specific categories of use. The Trade Marks Act 1996 states that a licence of a registered trade mark may be general, or may be limited, and that a limited licence may, in particular, apply:

(a) in relation to some, but not all, of the goods or services for which the trade mark is registered; or

(b) in relation to use of the trade mark in a particular manner or a particular locality (ss 32(1) and 32(2)).

Thus, a trade mark licence for a bar of chocolate may cover the manufacture and sale of chocolate under the mark, whereas a franchise agreement may licence the mark only for the use in retail sales of product sourced from the brand owner or authorised suppliers.

Similarly a copyright work can be licensed for some or all of the acts which, if carried out without consent, would constitute copyright infringement (eg, copying the work; making it available to the public; making an adaptation of the work).

Again, a patent can be licensed for some or all of the acts which, if carried out without consent, would constitute patent infringement. As you will know from previous chapters, the main acts which would infringe an Irish patent, if done without consent, are to make, dispose of (including sell), use or import the product. Where the patent is for a process, the main infringing acts are:

(a) to use the process; or

(b) to dispose of, use or import any product obtained directly by means of the process.

Again, the agreement can distinguish between the various 'infringing' acts, or alternatively use general wording. A licence to 'use and exploit' or 'use and exercise' the patent would probably have a general character encompassing all the 'infringing' acts.

In addition, the licence may be limited by reference to a particular technical field of application or product market. However, direct attempts to allocate customers between the licensor and the licensee within relevant markets or technical areas may raise competition law issues, especially if the licensor and licensee are competitors in that market or technical area when the licence is granted.

9.5.4 The scope of exclusivity

Is the licence to be exclusive, non-exclusive or sole? An exclusive licence means that the licensee has the right to use the licensed IP for the permitted purpose in the licensed territory, to the exclusion of all other parties, including to the exclusion of the licensor. This means that the licensor cannot itself use the licensed IP for the permitted purpose within the licensed territory, and it cannot grant any other licences to any third parties to do so.

A non-exclusive licence means that the licensor can use the licensed IP for the same permitted purpose in the same licensed territory, and can grant other licences to third parties to do the same.

A sole licence is an 'in-between' licence. It means that the licensor can use the licensed IP for the same permitted purpose in the same licensed territory, but that the licensor cannot grant any other licences to any third party to do so.

The scope of the licence does not need to be entirely exclusive, or entirely sole or non-exclusive. For example, the licensee could be granted an exclusive licence of the IP for the purposes of manufacturing licensed products in Ireland, and a non-exclusive licence of the IP for the purposes of marketing and selling these licensed products throughout the EU.

Although the above summarises the generally accepted meaning of the terms 'exclusive', 'non-exclusive' and 'sole' under Irish law, it can be difficult to determine exactly what is meant by these terms in any given context. It is therefore advisable to clearly define these terms in the agreement, in order to avoid any ambiguity in the future.

In order to fall within the TTBE, an exclusive licence of a patent or of know-how must be limited in time. Under a pure patent licence, for example, the exemption runs, in each country, for the life of the patent. In the case of pure know-how licence, the exemption is, in the main, limited to 10 years or less, depending on when the know-how was first exploited.

9.5.5 The territorial scope of the agreement

The agreement should specify the territory where the licensee can use the licensed IP for the permitted purpose. In some cases, a licensee may be subject to a number of territorial restrictions (eg, to manufacture only in certain territories, and to sell only in certain other territories).

Prohibitions on exploiting the licensed IP in certain territories is clearly restrictive of competition. However, the TTBE permits certain territorial restrictions to be placed on the licensee, namely:

(a) Territory of the licensor:
- a prohibition on the licensee in respect of the exploitation of the licensed technology in the territory of the licensor within the common market.

(b) Territories which are licensed to other licensees:
- a prohibition on the licensee in respect of the manufacture or use of the licensed product, or use of the licensed process, in territories within the common market which are licensed to other licensees;
- a prohibition on the licensee in respect of pursuing active sales endeavours in those territories; and
- a prohibition on the licensee in respect of satisfying unsolicited orders from those territories – ie, a prohibition on passive sales.

(Each of the above prohibitions can only continue for specific periods of time. For example, the prohibition with respect to satisfying unsolicited orders cannot continue for longer than five years from the date when the licensed product is first put on the market within the common market by any of the licensees.)

Where a licensee is prohibited from exploiting the licensed IP in certain territories, this is often specifically prohibited in the agreement, by including provisions which deal with each of the above four prohibitions.

When drafting the territorial restrictions in a licence agreement, it is also important to remember the EC law principle of 'exhaustion of rights'. Briefly, under this principle, (insofar as it relates to trade marks) where a product to which a trade mark has been applied is placed on the market in any country of the EU, with the consent of the trade mark owner, then that specific product is free to move and be re-sold in any other country within the EU, and the trade mark owner cannot rely on his trade mark rights in another Member State to prevent the parallel importation of that product. (Like the UK, Ireland has adopted the Trade Marks Harmonisation Directive 89/104/EEC of 21 December 1988 through the enactment of the Trade Marks Act 1996. Article 7 of the Directive, which outlines the principle of exhaustion of rights, is encompassed in s 16 of the Trade Marks Act 1996.) The same applies to products which are the subject of a patent or copyright. As regards patents, see, for example, *Merck & Co Inc v Stephar BV* [1981] ECR 2063; *Pharmon BV v Hoescht AG* [1985] ECR 2281; *Van Zuylen Frères v Hag AG* [1974] ECR 731. For copyright, see *Deutsche Grammophon Gesellschaft mbH v Metro* [1971] ECR 487.

At the heart of the principle of exhaustion of rights is the EU principle of free movement of goods. The TTBE specifically identifies provisions (in respect of patent and know-how licences) which would restrict such movement of products within the EU, as being blacklisted provisions and which would therefore fall foul of competition law rules.

9.5.6 Right to sub-contract and/or sub-licence

The agreement should specify whether the licensee is granted a 'have made' right – ie, whether the licensee can permit third parties to use the licensed IP for the manufacture of certain products on the licensee's behalf, and, if so, on what basis.

The agreement should also specify whether the licensee is permitted to grant sub-licences of the licensed IP. In this regard, it should be noted that the right of a licensee to grant sub-licences of its interest is subject to applicable law. For example, the Trade Marks Act 1996 states that a sub-licence may be granted by the licensee 'where the licence so provides' (s 32(5) Trade Marks Act 1996), ie, the right to sub-licence is not automatic.

Where a licensee is granted the right to sub-licence and/or a 'have made' right, this is often subject to certain conditions. For example, the agreement may require that the licensor be joined as a party to any such sub-licence or sub-contract agreement, or that the sub-licensee provide a direct covenant to the licensor, enabling the licensor to take action directly against the sub-licensee or sub-contractor in the event of any breach by the sub-licensee or sub-contractor of the sub-licence or sub-contract agreement. In addition, it would be usual for the agreement to provide that the licensee is at all times responsible for the activities of its sub-licensees or sub-contractors, and that the licensee is obliged to indemnify the licensor in respect of any of the activities of such sub-licensees or sub-contractors.

9.5.7 Assignability

It would be usual for a licensor to insist that the licensee is prohibited from assigning any of its rights or obligations under the agreement to a third party. In some instances, the licensor may permit a licensee to assign its rights or obligations to a subsidiary of the licensee.

Similarly, a licensee may wish to seek to prohibit the licensor from assigning any of its rights or obligations to any third party. It should be noted that, in certain circumstances, the acquirer of the IP may automatically continue to be bound by licences which were granted by a previous owner of the IP.

9.5.8 Term of the licence and renewal provisions

Patent licences (including 'mixed' licences, ie, licences of both patents and know-how) are normally expressed to run for the life of the patents being licensed. They may, however, be shorter.

There is no particular standard period for a know-how licence, although it is the common view that the commercial value of know-how reduces over time. The TTBE sets specific limits on the duration of the category exemption granted for territorial restrictions placed on a licensee of know-how. This has tended to result in pure know-how licences being granted for periods of 10 years or less.

Trade mark licences are not inherently limited in this way, and there is no reason why trade mark licences should not be granted without limit of time, or on a perpetually renewable basis. Having said this, there can be situations where competition law issues might arise (eg, in respect of a long term licence where the licence is exclusive or has other restrictive aspects). The question of whether competition law issues arise must be considered on a case-by-case basis.

Copyright licences can run for the copyright term, or any shorter period of time.

Where a licence agreement includes a right to renew the licence after the initial term, conditions will usually be laid down, eg, that the licensee has not been in breach of the agreement, etc. The renewal provisions may provide that the licence will only be renewed if one party gives the other party written notice, at least 30/60 days before the date of expiry of the licence, that it wishes to renew the licence. Alternatively, the agreement may provide that the licence will automatically renew, unless either party gives the other party written notice, at least 30/60 days before the date of expiry of the licence, that it does not wish to renew the licence. The renewal provisions should also state whether the licence, when renewed, will continue on the same terms, or whether the parties can vary the terms of the licence (eg, the royalty provisions).

9.5.9 Termination provisions

There may be circumstances where one or both of the parties intend certain provisions of the agreement to continue after termination of the IP licence itself (eg, the indemnity and confidentiality provisions). In view of this, the language dealing with termination should specifically distinguish between termination of the licence, and termination of the agreement.

The agreement will usually provide that either party may terminate the licence in the event that the other party is in breach of the agreement, and fails to remedy that breach within, say, 30 days of receipt of written notice of the breach by the non-breaching party. In some cases, the parties agree that this provision will only relate to material breaches which are incapable of remedy, in order to introduce some level of materiality to this termination event.

In addition, the agreement will usually provide that either party may terminate the licence in the event that the other party goes into liquidation or is the subject of any similar insolvency event, or in the event of a change of the corporate control of the other party.

The agreement may also provide that the licensor will be permitted to terminate the licence in the event that the licensee fails to pay sums due within the specified timelines, or fails to meet specified minimum sales targets, or in the event that the licensee challenges the validity of the licensed rights, or the secrecy or substantial nature of any licensed know-how.

For a licensee, termination of the licence is usually an event which it wishes to avoid at all costs. It may, therefore, seek to 'soften' the termination events, to give itself as many opportunities as possible to avoid termination of the licence.

It should be noted that the Patents Act 1992 provides that, irrespective of any contractual agreement to the contrary, a licence of a patent may be terminated by three months' notice in writing in the event that the relevant patent ceases to be in force (s 83(3)).

One aspect of a licence agreement which is often forgotten is the provision dealing with post-termination. First, the agreement should list those provisions which are to continue after termination of the licence (eg, confidentiality obligations; indemnity provisions). The agreement should also provide that, on termination of the licence for whatever reason, the licensee will forthwith return to the licensor all materials comprising any of the licensed IP, and will cease all use of the licensed IP for whatever reason. Also, the licensee should undertake to execute all documents and do all things that are reasonably necessary to ensure that all rights in the licensed IP and all goodwill in any licensed trade marks are owned by the licensor. The agreement should also deal with any existing stock of products manufactured using the licensed IP, ie, whether the licensee is permitted to sell all existing stock, provided it pays the licensor royalties in respect of same, or whether it is obliged to deliver all existing stock to the licensor as soon as the licence terminates.

9.5.10 Consideration/payment provisions

The provisions dealing with consideration or payments are very important, from the perspective of both the licensor and the licensee.

Licensors can be rewarded for the grant of a licence of IP in numerous ways, including the grant-back of a licence of IP from the licensee, or the payment of money by the licensee. The nature of the consideration will entirely depend on the circumstances of each arrangement, and will vary from agreement to agreement.

Where the consideration takes the form of payments, again, payments can take a number of different forms. For example, the licensee may pay a lump sum on execution of the licence, and then other payments during the term of the agreement. Identifying the preferred payment structure very much depends on the nature of the licensed IP, and on whether you are acting for the licensor or the licensee.

For example, a licensee may prefer to negotiate royalty payments over the term of the licence. Royalties are usually calculated as a percentage of the annual aggregate net sales price achieved by the licensee in selling quantities of products which incorporate any of the licensed IP. The term 'net sales price' must be defined very clearly, in order to remove any ambiguity as to how the royalties are calculated (eg, whether it includes all income actually received by the licensee from the sale of products, or all income receivable by the licensee from the sale of products). A licensee may prefer this form of consideration as it reduces the likelihood of the licensee making a loss from the arrangement, in that the licensee only has to pay sums to the licensor where the licensee actually makes sales of the products. Where an agreement provides for royalties to be paid, it should also specifically deal with the sale of products to affiliates of the licensee, and with the sale of products by sub-licensees and sub-contractors.

A licensor, on the other hand, may not be happy with this royalty structure, and may wish to include a minimum royalty which the licensee must pay to it annually, irrespective of the number of products sold by the licensee. A minimum annual royalty gives the licensor comfort, as the licensor is guaranteed to receive at least this sum each year, in respect of the licence, even if the licensee does not sell many products.

9.5.11 Ownership of improvements

Where a licensee creates improvements to the licensed IP, the licensor will naturally wish to have access to those improvements. However, the TTBE specifically blacklists any provision which obliges a licensee to assign any improvements which it makes to the licensor. The most a licensor can seek, in order to fall within the TTBE, is to oblige the licensee to grant the licensor a licence of any improvements. Further, this obligation can only be placed on the licensee if the licensor itself is also obliged to grant the licensee a licence of any improvements it makes.

The TTBE goes on to provide that, where the improvements created by the licensee are what it terms, 'severable improvements', the licensee cannot be obliged to grant an exclusive licence of such improvements to the licensor, but rather can only be obliged to grant a non-exclusive licence of them. There is a view that, as the TTBE does not specifically prohibit it, where the improvements created by the licensee are not severable from the licensed IP, the licensor can oblige the licensee to grant an exclusive licence of such improvements.

However, this view has not been tested. Further, the concept of 'severable' and 'non-severable' improvements may be difficult to apply, as indeed may the concept of 'improvements' in general, as none of these terms are defined in the TTBE.

9.5.12 Warranties

The licence agreement will often contain warranties from the licensor. These are designed to give the licensee comfort with respect to key facts underlying the transaction and/or to allocate risk. Standard warranties may be included dealing with matters such as corporate authority or capacity, but there are also likely to be IP-specific warranties. The following are some examples:

(a) that the licensor is the owner of the licensed IP, or, if it is not the owner, that it has a valid right to sub-licence the licensed IP to the licensee on the terms of the agreement. Where the licensor is not in fact the owner of the licensed IP, the licensee should carry out investigations in respect of the actual owner of the licensed IP, and the terms of the licence agreement between the owner of the licensed IP and the licensor;

(b) where any of the licensed IP comprises registered IP, or applications for registrations, that they are valid (so far as the licensor is aware) and in force, and that all fees in respect of such applications or registrations have been paid;

(c) that there is no current or threatened litigation connected with the licensed IP;

(d) that the use of the licensed IP by the licensee in the manner envisaged by the agreement will not (so far as the licensee is aware) infringe the IP rights of any third party. This is the most important issue which a licensee needs to deal with.

As you will see below, it is also important for a licensee to negotiate a comprehensive indemnity provision in respect of infringements of third party IP, if this is possible; and, where the licence is exclusive, that the licensor has not granted any licence of the licensed IP to any third party.

If no warranties are given, it would be usual for the agreement to specifically state this, as failure to do so could give rise to a risk that statutory or implied warranties apply.

9.5.13 Indemnities

It would be common for licence agreements to contain two forms of indemnities:

(a) *Indemnity from the licensor* in respect of any costs, claims or damages incurred by the licensee, by reason of any claim that the use by the licensee of the licensed IP infringes the IP rights of a third party.

(b) *Indemnity from the licensee* in respect of any costs, claims or damages incurred by the licensor as a result of any defects in products made under the licence, or as a result of any of the activities of the licensee, save for any costs, claims or damages for which the licensor is obliged to indemnify the licensee.

The question of whether either or both of these indemnities will be given, and the scope of these indemnities, depends very much on the nature of the IP rights being granted, and the other risks and rewards undertaken by or available to the parties under the agreement. Indemnities in respect of infringement of third party IP are more likely in relation to copyright or confidential information than in relation to patents, since the licensor is in a better position to know whether he has misappropriated copyright-protected, confidential or proprietary material than he has to evaluate the risks of a patent infringement claim.

Any indemnity given by the licensor will often be subject to a number of conditions (eg, the indemnity may only cover liability incurred through acts of the licensee that are wholly within the scope, terms and conditions of the licence).

9.5.14 Infringement claims against third parties

The agreement should deal with the rights and obligations of each of the parties in the event that any third party is suspected of infringing any of the licensed IP. In this regard, the following should be noted:

(a) The Trade Marks Act 1996 provides that, unless the licence of a registered trade mark (or any licence through which the licensee's interest is derived) provides otherwise, a licensee is entitled to call upon the proprietor of any registered trade mark which is licensed to it, to take infringement proceedings in respect of any matter which affects the licensee's interests. If the proprietor either refuses to take any such proceedings, or fails to do so within two months of being called upon to do so, then the licensee may bring the proceedings in his own name as if he were the proprietor (s 34(2) and (3)). See also remainder of s 34 and s 35 and s 36, which outline other rights of licensees with respect to taking registered trade mark infringement proceedings. It should be noted that a licensee will not have the protection under s 34 or s 35 unless the licence is recorded at the Irish Trade Mark Registry (see also section 9.2 above).

(b) The Patents Act 1992 provides that the holder of an exclusive patent licence has the same right as the patent owner to bring infringement proceedings in respect of any infringement of the patent committed after the date of the licence (s 51). It should be noted that, if the patent licence is not recorded at the Patents Registry, it shall only be admitted in any court as evidence of the licensee's interest in that patent, if the court so directs (s 85(7)).

(c) The Copyright and Related Rights Act 2000 provides that an exclusive licensee of copyright has, except as against the copyright owner, the same rights and remedies in respect of matters occurring after the grant of the licence as if the licence had been an assignment (s 135(1)). The Act also provides the same with respect to an exclusive licensee of databases (s 338).

The position with respect to the rights of licensees in the event of infringement of licensed IP varies from country to country, however, and it is therefore important that, where the agreement covers a multi-jurisdictional territory, the agreement deals in detail with the rights and obligations of the parties in these circumstances.

Where the licence is non-exclusive, it is less likely that the agreement will grant the licensee a right to take infringement proceedings itself. Where the licence is exclusive, however, the licensee may seek the right to take certain action in the event of the licensed

IP being infringed, and at the least, may seek to place strict obligations on the licensor to take action in such circumstances.

9.5.15 Confidentiality

Each party should undertake to keep all confidential information of the other party strictly confidential at all times, and to only use same for the purposes permitted under the agreement. The confidentiality provision will often specify the categories of individuals to whom the confidential information can be disclosed (ie, employees, sub-contractors, consultants, etc).

It is important that the term 'confidential information' is clearly defined, and includes all licensed IP and improvements to same.

Standard carve-out provisions will also be included, providing that the confidentiality obligation does not apply to information that is in the public domain (or which subsequently enters into the public domain through no fault of the receiving party), and will allow for any disclosure necessary to comply with a court order.

9.5.16 Obligations of licensor

The obligations placed on the licensor will very much depend on the nature of the licensed IP, and the proposed activities of the licensee in respect of the licensed IP. Having said this, however, the following are some obligations which a licensee will often seek from a licensor:

(a) to pay all fees in respect of patent, trade mark and registered designs registrations and applications during the term of the licence, and not to do, or fail to do, anything which would allow them to lapse; and

(b) to provide technical assistance to the licensee for, say, the first six months of the licence.

9.5.17 Obligations of licensee

Again, the obligations placed on the licensee will very much depend on the nature of the licensed IP, and the proposed activities of the licensee in respect of the licensed IP. For example, where the licensee will be manufacturing products, an obligation is often placed on it to observe minimum quality specifications, and to permit the licensor to inspect the products at any time on giving fair notice. In order to fall within the TTBE, any obligation placed on the licensee to observe minimum quality specifications must be limited to the extent that such a requirement is necessary either for a technically proper exploitation of the licensed IP, or to ensure that the licensed product conforms to the minimum quality specifications that are applicable to the licensor and other licensees.

Irrespective of the nature of the licensed IP, the following are some obligations which will usually be placed on the licensee:

(a) at all times to make it clear to third parties that it is using the licensed IP under licence from the licensor, and to affix such patent, trade marks and/or copyright notices (as applicable) to its products as the licensor may request;

(b) to notify the licensor as soon as it becomes aware of any suspected or threatened infringement by any third party of the licensed IP; and

(c) to maintain detailed records relating to its sales of licensed products, and to make same available for inspection upon the reasonable request of the licensor.

One of the main obligations placed on a licensee will be to use either its 'reasonable' or its 'best' endeavours to properly exploit the licensed IP. There has been substantial case law as to the meaning of the terms 'reasonable endeavours' and 'best endeavours'. From this case law it is clear that the term 'best endeavours' places a substantially high level of obligation on the licensee. The obligation to use 'best endeavours' is often found in an agreement where the licensee is granted a level of exclusivity in respect of the licensed IP, either in respect of its use of the licensed IP, or the territorial scope of the licence.

In addition to, or in the alternative to, placing an obligation on the licensee to use its reasonable or best endeavours to exploit the licensed IP, the licensor can specify certain minimum sales targets which the licensee must meet each year, or alternatively, can provide for a minimum royalty. Minimum sales targets or royalty payments can be drafted in such a way as to take into account the fact that the licensee may not be in a position to exploit the licensed IP straight away. For example, the agreement could provide for an incremental minimum sales target, or a sales target that only commences after, say, the first two years of the licence term.

9.5.18 Governing law, jurisdiction, dispute resolution

As with all agreements, the provisions dealing with governing law, jurisdiction and dispute resolution should be considered carefully. When drafting dispute resolution provisions, there are various options available, and you should discuss these with your client in order to ascertain the provision which is most appropriate to meet the needs of your client.

9.6 The tax treatment of licensing of intellectual property

9.6.1 Withholding tax

Sections 237 and 238 of the Taxes Consolidation Act 1997 (TCA) deal with the withholding tax treatment of, *inter alia*, any royalty or other sum paid in respect of the user of a patent. Section 237 of the TCA only applies to payments wholly out of profits or gains bought into charge to income tax. Section 238 of the TCA applies to payments made by Irish resident companies and provides that on payment of any royalty or other sum paid in respect of the user of a patent, the person by or through whom any such payment is made shall deduct out of the payment a sum representing the amount of income tax on the payment at the standard rate of tax in force at the time of payment. Thus the obligation to deduct tax under s 238 of the TCA is mandatory where there is a payment of a royalty or other sum in respect of the user of a patent.

Section 237 of the TCA provides that where any annuity or other annual payment is payable out of profits or gains brought into charge to income tax, then withholding tax may be applied by the payer. Section 238 of the TCA similarly applies to the payment of any annuity or other annual payment charged with tax under Sched D, but the application of withholding tax is mandatory under s 238 of the TCA.

Thus, in determining whether withholding tax applies to any licensing of IP, one must consider whether the payment is annual payment or whether the payment is in respect of the user of a patent.

9.6.2 VAT treatment of IP licences

The exploitation of intangible property for the purposes of obtaining income from such property on a continuing basis is regarded as an 'economic activity' for VAT purposes in accordance with the provisions of Art 4 of the Sixth Council Directive (77/388/EEC). Accordingly, the exploitation of IP on a royalty or other basis will be regarded as an activity subject to VAT if undertaken within an EU Member State. Schedule 4 to the VAT Act 1972 provides that transfers and assignments of copyrights, patents, licences, trade marks and similar rights are taxable for VAT purposes where they are received. Whilst Sched 4 to the VAT Act 1972 specifies that transfers and assignments of IP are taxable where received, for VAT purposes a licence is regarded as an ongoing assignment of IP for the licence period. Thus licences of IP are treated as taxable where the service is received.

9.6.3 Stamp duty

Whilst an assignment of IP may be liable to stamp duty under the head of charge 'Conveyance or Transfer on Sale', the grant of an exclusive licence may also be chargeable to stamp duty under this head of charge. The grant of an exclusive, irrevocable licence to use an Irish patent (even if restricted as to territory) for the life of the patent for consideration is normally chargeable to Irish stamp duty as a Conveyance on Sale. There is, however, very little commentary or case law underpinning the stamp duty treatment of licences of patents. It is also unclear whether similar treatment would apply to other licences of IP, for example copyright.

It should be noted that, in order to record an assignment of a patent or trade mark at the Irish Patent and Trade Marks Registry, or in order to introduce it as evidence in court proceedings, the assignment must be stamped by the Revenue Commissioners.

9.6.4 IP licence fees

In general, the treatment of profits or gains derived from the licensing of IP will depend on whether the profits or gains are regarded as income or capital for tax purposes and on the tax residence of the licensor.

However, Irish tax legislation taxes as income all types of profits or gains derived from a patent and from any rights under a patent. This treatment applies irrespective of whether the receipt in respect of the licensing of a patent is of an income or capital nature. Irish tax legislation further provides that where a capital sum is received from the sale (including licensing) of patent rights, then this amount may be taxed over a period of six years, ie one-sixth of the capital sum is taxable each year for a six-year period. Alternatively, the person in receipt of the capital sum may elect for the entire amount to be taxed in the period in which the sum is received. In the case of non-Irish tax residents, the entire capital amount received is taxable as income in the year it is received unless the person elects for the amount to be taxed over a six-year period (s 757(2) of the TCA).

There are no similar provisions in the case of licences of other types of IP. Thus, the applicable tax treatment will depend, as stated above, on the tax residence status of the licensor and on the characterisation of the profits or gains as income or capital.

CHAPTER 10

CONFIDENTIAL INFORMATION

Carol Plunkett

10.1 Introduction

In certain instances where the laws relating to copyright, patents, trade marks and contractual obligations do not protect against the unauthorised use of information or of a concept, the courts have held that a duty to preserve such a confidence may be imposed. This is a difficult area of the law, in that, because it is entirely 'judge-made' and very much based on equitable principles, there are a number of uncertainties and, indeed, some of the cases contradict each other. However, most of the case law agrees that there are three essential requirements to satisfy a claim for breach of confidence:

(a) The first element is that the owner of the confidential information must establish that the information which he seeks to protect is in fact confidential, that is, that it has the necessary quality of confidence about it. The information must be inaccessible to the public, although as we shall see later it need not be something which a third party or a member of the public could not compile themselves.

(b) The second essential element is that the confidential information must have been imparted in circumstances which imposed an obligation of confidence on the person receiving it.

(c) Thirdly, the person alleging that a breach of confidence has occurred must be able to show that the person of whom he complains has breached that obligation and has used the information in a manner that was not intended by its owner and is not authorised by him.

10.2 Why should confidential information be protected?

Paul Lavery in his book, *Commercial Secrets* (1996, Roundhall, Sweet & Maxwell) includes a very good quotation from Robert A Spanner's book *Who Owns Innovation – The Rights and Obligations of Employers and Employees*, published in 1984 in the US, as follows:

> The old adage 'knowledge is power' is coming to have its commercial counterpart in the more sordid but equally valid aphorism 'information is money'. In a nation that is entering the so-called post-industrial information society, information has quite literally become Capital.

This quote could sum up a lot of what has been discussed in the chapters of this text. The dependence of economies on possession of land or machinery and the importance of that dependence is now out-weighed by the importance of dependence upon what might be called 'intellectual capital'. Economies which have the knowledge to produce things more efficiently, to develop new technology to do this and to improve efficiency overall, gain the competitive edge. Intellectual capital or, quite simply, ideas, are paramount in this. As soon as an idea is shared with a third party, it is open to attack. It is essential that commercial secrets can be protected against disclosure and that the courts impose this obligation to hold such information confidential.

Obviously, if this prohibition on releasing information had no exceptions, then economies would stagnate, and so the courts have balanced these two opposite ends of the spectrum. In general, the court will not allow information which has been disclosed in confidence to be used in a way that is inconsistent with the purpose for which the information was imparted. Neither will the courts allow use of information which was stolen from its owner.

On the other hand, no one will be prevented from using information which is already in the public domain. If someone can prove that they have independently carried out their own research in developing a product, the courts will not grant an injunction stopping them from using that product even if it has already been developed by another company. No one can be stopped from 'reverse engineering' a product; that is, no one can be stopped from purchasing at market value any product in the market place and working backwards to find out how it is manufactured. Obviously, if patent protection exists in respect of the product, this is a different matter, since it cannot be made without licence of the owner of the patent, but in all other cases reverse engineering is permitted. Furthermore, the courts have always allowed an employee to use his skill and experience which he has gained while employed; this is as opposed to using the secrets of his former employer.

10.3 History

Lavery refers to the world's oldest written code of laws, the Hammurabic code of 2100 BC, which apparently ordered the loss of an eye for those who were caught with forbidden secrets.

In Roman law, an action existed in relation to the corruption of a slave, which arose most often where a Roman citizen had persuaded the slave of a competitor to give him his master's commercial secrets. Prior to the 18th century, the government in England took a very paternalistic attitude and the economy was strictly regulated. The Guilds, referred to in Chapter 1 ante, which were set up to govern various trades, had strict rules setting out who could receive certain information or trade secrets. During the 18th and 19th centuries, however, economic policy became permissive and *laissez-faire* was the order of the day. The City and Guilds groups became less powerful and the restrictive legislation was repealed.

As a result, tradespeople and manufacturers had to seek new remedies and the courts gradually introduced the action for breach of confidence.

Cases are reported as far back as the 1730s and the 1750s. In *Webb v Rose* (1732) 98 ER 924 an injunction was granted to stop the defendant from printing the plaintiff's father's drafts. In *Pope v Curl* (1741) 26 ER 608, Mr Pope obtained an injunction restraining Mr Curl, a bookseller, from selling a book called *Letters from Swift, Pope and Others* as long as the book contained letters in Mr Pope's name.

Although initially the action for breach of confidence related to information in written form, over the years the law advanced and protected not just matters of copyright, but specifically, the underlying confidence of the information which was imparted. In Chapter 1 ante, the case of *Prince Albert v Strange* (1849) 1 Mac & G 25 was mentioned, where the defendants were stopped from publishing etchings owned by the Royal Family, which had been left with a printer to have copies made.

In addition to numerous employment cases where confidential information has been considered, the courts have had to consider cases where no employment relationship exists between the parties. These cases have required the courts to strike a fair balance between the right to confidentiality alleged by the plaintiff as against, in Ireland, our constitutional right to convey information to the public.

Over the years, these two main circumstances, that of an 'unemployment' situation and an employment relationship, have evolved.

One manner of describing confidential information is to use the term 'know-how'. 'Know-how' can be secret formulae, it can be processes in manufacturing, or it could also be simple things like lists of names of customers and sales information. This category was referred to earlier, when it was said that the information need not necessarily be secret. It can be information which has been gathered and is preserved in a particular manner by its owner.

Over the years, the court has divided information into three categories. The first of these is trivia or public information. This information is not protected and there can be no duty to hold it confidential.

The second category of information is skill and experience. This is not protected in ordinary circumstances, but it could be restricted in, for example, a contract of employment, by a restriction of trade clause. Clearly, restriction of trade clauses are a difficult area, since an employee has a constitutional right to be able to leave one employment and commence another, and to use certain aspects of the skill and experience which he has gained in one employment in furtherance of his career. Having said that, the courts will impose an obligation on an employee to comply with a reasonable restriction of trade clause. So, cases which prohibit trading in a certain area for a particular length of time can be regarded as reasonable.

The third type of information is that of trade secrets and the courts have found that irrespective of any written obligation, an employee has an obligation to hold trade secrets safe even after he has left a particular employer.

Because this area of the law is judge- and case-driven, the best way of explaining how the law of confidential information has evolved is to discuss several of the more interesting cases and for this purpose they have been divided in this chapter into two categories. The first category is that of non-employment cases and the second category is that of employment cases where an employee has been sued for setting up business in competition with a former employer allegedly using trade secrets owned by that former employer.

10.3.1 The non-employment cases

Turning to the first category, the non-employment cases, the first case which deserves mention is that of *Saltman Engineering v Campbell Engineering* [1948] 65 RPC 203; [1963] 2 All ER 413. Lord Greene gave judgment in this case and his judgment is often cited in later cases. The facts of this case were that Campbell Engineering made tools for leather punching for Saltman Engineering, based on drawings which were provided by Saltman. The relationship broke down and after Saltman and Campbell parted company, the defendants continued to manufacture and market leather punches. The plaintiff claimed that this was an abuse of the confidential information contained in the drawings, which had been provided to Campbell Engineering. The court agreed. The defendants claimed that there was no secret in the drawings. They could after all have gone out and bought any of the Saltman punches, dismantled them, drawn specifications and reverse engineered them. While the judge did not disagree with this, his concern was that by using the drawings, the defendants had saved themselves a substantial amount of time, rather than investing the time and effort which should have been necessary to produce their own punches. Lord Greene said:

> The information to be protected must have the necessary quality of confidence about it. That is, it must not be something which is public property or public knowledge, but it is perfectly possible to have a confidential document which is the result of work done by its

maker on materials which are available to anyone. What makes the document secret is that its maker used his brain to come up with the results which it contains and this produced a result which could only have been produced by someone going through the same process.

In *Terrapin v Builders Supply (Hayes) and Others* [1960] RPC 128 which was decided in 1960, the plaintiff had been using the defendant company to market portable buildings for them, and during negotiations had disclosed details of an updated version that they were designing. The relationship broke down. The defendants began to make their own portable buildings including some of the updating features which had been discussed with them by the plaintiff. The plaintiff sought an injunction for abuse of confidential information and it was granted by Roxburgh J. He said:

> I understand the essence of this branch of the law, whatever the origin of it may be, is that a person which has obtained information in confidence is not allowed to use it as a springboard for activities detrimental to the person who made the confidential communication and springboard it remains even when all the features have been published or can be ascertained by actual inspection by members of the public. The dismantling of a unit might enable a person to proceed without plans or specifications or other technical information but not, I think, without some of the know-how and certainly not without taking the trouble to dismantle.

He goes on to say that it is his view that the processor of such information must be placed under a special disability in the field of competition, in order to ensure that he does not get an unfair start.

There were two *Seager v Copydex* cases ((No 1) [1967] 2 All ER 415; (No 2) [1969] 2 All ER 718). These cases involved the manufacture of carpet grips by Seager and which were marketed by Copydex. At one meeting Mr Seager disclosed details of another idea which he had, for a corner grip. Mr Seager explained the design, showed drawings and specifications, and explained its advantage over existing carpet grips on the market. Relations broke down. Copydex brought a grip onto the market. Although Mr Seager had a patent, it was found that Copydex was not infringing it. However, Lord Denning said that although he believed Copydex when they said they did not consciously abuse Seager's secrets, the court found that the two products were so strikingly similar that Copydex must unconsciously have used the information which Seager had disclosed at the meetings. Lord Denning applied the 'springboard' principle, that a person who has obtained information in confidence is not to use it as a springboard for activities detrimental to the person who made the confidential information and springboard remains even when all the knowledge has become public. The later *Seager v Copydex* case ((No 2) [1969] 2 All ER 718) dealt with the principles on which damages were to be assessed and held that they should be assessed on the market value of the information as between a willing buyer and willing seller. The case further said that, while damages were assessed and paid, the property and the confidential information vested in the defendant company and it had a right to make use of it.

Coco v Clarke [1969] RPC 41 set out the essentials of the doctrine of confidential information, those which were mentioned at the beginning of this chapter:

(a) the information itself must have the necessary quality of confidence about it;
(b) the circumstances in which the information was imparted must have imported confidentiality; and
(c) there must have been unauthorised use of information to the detriment of the imparting party.

The facts of that case are that Coco invented a Moped and he approached the defendant to make it. He showed them a prototype, specifications and drawings. The relationship broke down. Clarke said they were going to use their own design, because there were too many problems with Coco's design. When the Clarke Moped came on the market, Coco believed it was not a new invention, but had been manufactured by use of the know-how he had disclosed. The defendants agreed to keep an account and pay a royalty of 5 shillings per engine up to the trial so that no injunction was granted.

Then there are two Irish cases worth looking at. The first is *Oblique Financial Services v Promise Production Company Ltd* (1994) 1 PLRM 74 and this involved the *Phoenix* magazine. The plaintiff was a company partly owned by a lady named Mary Breen-Farrelly. It organised financial support for film production and entered into a contract with the Promise Production company to finance a film. The name of the investor was to be held secret and unfortunately, the *Phoenix* published an article to the effect that the Roman Catholic Church was the investor, commenting that this was a rather unusual investment for such a body. This case came before the Irish court as an application under s 11 of the Jurisdiction of Courts and Enforcement of Judgments Act, for 'an order in aid' of proceedings, which had taken place in the UK. The court held that the obligation of confidentiality which is enforced by the courts is not merely applicable to parties to a contract, but also in relation to third parties who may also come into possession of that information.

The court enforced the obligation of confidentiality of the company against *Phoenix* magazine. This was in spite of the fact that the defendants argued that granting an injunction would infringe the constitutional rights of the *Phoenix* magazine as an organ or opinion under Art 40 of the Constitution. However, the court said that this is not an absolute right, but one which is qualified having regard to other legal constraints. It should be remembered that this was an interlocutory injunction and the matter was settled afterwards, but it was interesting nonetheless.

The last case in this category is *National Irish Bank v RTE* [1998] 2 IR 465. This involved the proposed disclosure by RTE of a certain tax structure, which apparently allowed investors in a particular scheme to evade their tax liabilities. The bank argued that publication of details in relation to this would irreparably damage the relationship of trust and confidence between the bank and their customers and would result in a loss of customers. They denied that there was any wrongdoing in relation to the operation of the scheme. It was common case that the information was confidential and so the court had to decide the balance of the public interest in preserving confidences as against the public interest in favour of disclosure of serious wrongdoings. At the interlocutory stage, Shanley J discharged the *ex parte* injunction which had been granted, and this was upheld by the Supreme Court which said that information concerning allegations of tax evasion was a matter of genuine interest and importance to the general public, and in the public interest, the general public should be given the information.

10.3.2 The employment cases

Turning to the employment cases, the first of these cases to consider is one called *Meadox Medicals v VPI Ltd and Denis Cummings and George Goicoechea* (High Court, 27 April 1982, unreported). This is a case which was heard before Mr Justice Hamilton in 1981. Mr Cummings and Dr Goicoechea had worked for Meadox Medicals in the US, and during that employment had access to know-how and trade secrets relating to the development of what was called a woven double velour graft which was used as a replacement artery.

These gentlemen resigned from Meadox Medicals, became employees of a French company, left that company and within a year of having left Meadox Medicals, had set up their own company in Shannon manufacturing arterial prostheses. The court gave a lengthy judgment and was satisfied that it was 'highly improbable if not inconceivable' that the product could have been conceived within the time without the benefit and knowledge and confidential data required by Dr Goicoechea and Denis Cummings in the course of their employment by the plaintiff. Both gentlemen had signed confidentiality agreements with Meadox and the court was satisfied that they were in breach of those agreements.

In *Faccenda Chicken v Fowler* [1985] 1 All ER 724, the plaintiff sold fresh chickens and in 1973 employed Mr Fowler as a sales manager. At his suggestion, the company adopted a method of selling fresh chickens from refrigerated vans. Over the years, sales information, customers' names and addresses, routes and prices charged and so on were gathered. In 1980, Mr Fowler left and set up his own business in exactly the same area, doing exactly the same thing, together with five of the salesmen from Faccenda Chicken. None of the employees had a restrictive covenant in their employment contract. Goulding J, who heard the case, said that there were three categories of information, those which we have already discussed:

- trivia or public information which is not protected;
- skill and experience which is not protected but can be restricted by contract;
- trade secrets which are protected.

He found that Fowler and the others had acquired skill and experience, not secret information, and he refused to grant an injunction.

The second last case is *Lawrence David Ltd v Ashton* [1991] 1 All ER 385. In this case, the plaintiffs manufactured vehicle bodies and employed Mr Ashton as a sales director. His contract of employment said that he would not, during or after employment, disclose to anyone any information relating to the plaintiffs or their customers or divulge any trade secrets, and that he would not be involved for two years after his employment in the design, development, manufacture or supply of similar products. Mr Ashton was fired and he went to work for a competitor. The plaintiffs sought damages for breach of contract and an injunction to stop Mr Ashton's use of confidential information and to enforce the restraint of trade clause. The Court of Appeal refused the injunction against disclosing confidential information, because it was not possible to define the confidential information or the trade secrets which the plaintiff sought to protect.

This case makes it clear that it is very important that the employee knows precisely what it is he may and may not do, and emphasises the importance of clarity in the drafting of such contracts.

The last case, which is possibly the most important case in Ireland on this topic, is *House of Spring Gardens v Point Blank Ltd* [1984] IR 611. This case involves the development of a bullet-proof vest by an inventor who entered into agreements with Point Blank Ltd to manufacture the vests for him. Relationships broke down. It was agreed that the inventor would get royalties from any further contract of the supply of vests by Point Blank Ltd, particularly to the Libyan Authorities. The defendant did not pay any royalties. The inventor claimed for breach of contract and copyright, but also claimed an injunction for breach of know-how and abuse of confidential information. Costello J granted the injunction and the Supreme Court upheld his decision. Costello J's judgment gives a very good analysis of the UK cases and points out that he is enunciating the law in Ireland in relation to confidential information for the first time. Costello J's rules are, first, decide if there is a relationship between the parties which imports confidence, and second, decide whether the information can properly be recorded as confidential.

10.4 Remedies

A brief note in relation to remedies for breach of confidential information. Clearly, because this is an equitable solution to an equitable problem, the first thing to consider is an application for an injunction. In all applications for injunctions, but particularly in this area, speed is of the essence. If your client comes to you some months after the employee has left, then in all likelihood you will not be granted an injunction and should not waste your client's money seeking one. Obviously, if you have clear evidence that either documentation or computer files have been stolen, then your client's case may be strengthened. However, you will still have to prove that the balance of probability lies with the plaintiff, that there is a stateable case and that damages do not constitute an adequate remedy.

Consider the seeking of a Mareva injunction, that is one to freeze all bank accounts, etc, and perhaps an Anton Piller order where you are permitted to go and remove any documentation which may be relevant to the issues in order to preserve it until the trial.

In relation to damages, at the plaintiff's option, these can be either a straightforward amount of money in damages or an account of profits made by the defendant. The case law, after a great deal of discussion, appears to be in favour of awarding the plaintiff damages which would be the amount of money the defendant would have spent in gathering the information and the profit the defendant has made as a result of the springboard advantage he had.

CHAPTER 11

CONCLUSION

Maureen Daly

11.1 Introduction

By the time the reader reaches this chapter, I hope that they have come to the conclusion that intellectual property plays an important role in today's environment, both at a national and international level.

As already mentioned in earlier chapters, intellectual property is personal property and is an asset that can be exploited by means of assignments, licences and mortgages. No one would argue against this exploitation as it contributes to improved competitiveness, employment and innovation. It is also a just reward for the time, effort and financial expenditure incurred by the proprietor in creating and developing the intellectual property.

However, as demonstrated in Chapter 1 by the tale of St Columcille, since time immemorial, individuals have copied the works of others and there is no doubt that this activity (whether deliberate or unintentional) will continue to take place. Therefore, it is important for proprietors of intellectual property rights (and their legal advisors) to be vigilant and to pursue infringers as and when they appear on the market. Such a pro-active approach is vital as it sends out a strong signal to other would-be infringers that such activities will not be tolerated and that the proprietor will pursue those that infringe its rights.

11.2 Future developments

Developments that are likely to arise in the future, while not discussed in this book, are detailed below and are issues that solicitors should monitor very closely.

11.3 Trade marks

Following the completion of accession negotiations on 12–13 December 2002 the European Union will be welcoming 10 new Member States as and from 1 May 2004. The candidate countries are Cyprus, the Czech Republic, Estonia, Hungary, Latvia, Lithuania, Malta, Poland, the Slovak Republic and Slovenia. It is anticipated that Bulgaria and Romania will join the European Union in 2007. The accession of these new Member States will have an impact on the community trade mark system, and, in advance of the enlargement of the European Union, the European Commission has issued a proposal for a Council Regulation amending Regulation EU/40/94 on the community trade mark (see COM (2002) 767). Much of the changes being proposed by the European Commission are procedural amendments to the community trade mark system. On a practical level, for those clients that currently possess community trade mark registrations or already have an application pending for such a mark, the enlargement of the European Union will have implications for them which all solicitors should be aware of.

Another topical issue is the question of 'International Exhaustion of Rights' (namely, the reliance by trade mark owners on a national or community-wide registration to prevent the importation of goods into the EEA from outside). It is beyond the ambit of this book to discuss this very complex issue, but suffice to say that this may, at some point, be addressed by the European Commission in the face of lobbying from interested parties such as consumer organisations.

On 21 January 2003, the European Commission issued a proposal for a Council Regulation (to replace Council Regulation EC/3295/94) concerning customs action against goods suspected of infringing certain intellectual property rights and the measures to be taken against goods found to have infringed such rights (COM (2003)). The new law would extend the powers of customs officials to allow them to take action against counterfeiters on their own initiative and without a formal claim from a company. It would also cover more intellectual property rights, such as plant variety rights, geographical indications and designations of origin. It would also abolish the fees that companies currently have to pay if they want customs to seize counterfeit products.

Finally, the European Commission intends to introduce a new Directive that would harmonise legislation on the enforcement of intellectual property rights across the European Union. On 30 January 2003, the provisional text for the proposal for such a Directive was issued by the European Commission. A review of this document reveals that the Member States will be obliged to provide for the proportionate measures and procedures needed to ensure the enforcement of intellectual property rights, which includes providing for provisional and precautionary measures to protect those rights as well as imposing penalties and awarding damages in circumstances where infringement has been deemed to have occurred. In cases of serious infringements, provision for criminal sanctions should exist. Also, Member States will be obliged to provide for appropriate legal protection against the manufacture, import, distribution and use of a device that manufactures goods which infringe the intellectual property rights of another and incorporates elements or signs which are recognised by customers, thereby making it easy to identify the goods as authentic. These are just some of the provisions of the provisional proposal. As the European Commission has not indicated when the final text of the proposal will be issued, caution should be had when reviewing the initial draft proposal as it may differ to the final version.

11.4 Patents

The introduction of a community patent system is now awaited following the agreement of the European Council in early March 2003 on a 'common political approach' to the community patent. This approach includes the main outlines of the system whereby a centralised court will rule on disputes, the language regime, costs and the role of National Patent Offices and the distribution of fees. A number of steps will have to be taken before the community patent system is operational, such as the adoption of the text of a proposed regulation on the community patent. Other areas where likely developments might occur at European and/or international levels are in respect of computer software and biotechnology.

11.5 Copyright

As already mentioned in Chapter 5 ante, the Directive on the harmonisation of certain aspects of copyright and related rights in the Information Society has yet to be implemented in Ireland. It is envisaged that its adoption will not require substantive changes to copyright legislation in Ireland.

11.6 Stamp duty

As intellectual property rights are a form of personal property, instruments which convey or transfer such property fall within the ambit of the stamp duty provisions of finance legislation. Submissions have been made to the government requesting that, similar to the position in the UK, stamp duty not be levied on such transfers. Given the practical implications of such a move for the proprietor of intellectual property rights, developments in this area should be monitored closely by solicitors.

11.7 Conclusion

For those solicitors advising national and international clients on intellectual property law, it is comforting to note that Ireland is in compliance with its European and international obligations. However, it is important for solicitors to closely monitor developments in the area so that they will be in a position to advise their clients of the implications (if any) of such changes.

INDEX

Broadcasting 5.2.2
   See Copyright

Computer programs 1.3, 2.2.4, 5.1.2,
                               5.1.5, 5.2.2, 6.1, 8.10
   See also Databases
   adaption, making an 7.1.8.3
   authorship 7.1.7
   central processing unit (CPU) 7.1.1
   definition of 7.1.5, 7.1.6
   developments at EU level 7.1.2
   distribution of 7.1.8.2
   international treaty law and 7.1.2
   language 7.1.1
   literary works as 7.1.2, 7.1.4, 7.1.5
      See also Copyright
   making available right 7.1.8.2
      See also Copyright
   ownership 7.1.7
   protection of 7.1–7.1.9.3
   reproduction right 7.1.8.1
      See also Copyright
   restricted acts 7.1.8
      exceptions to 7.1.9
         backup copies 7.1.9.1
         decompilation right 7.1.9.2
         incidental acts 7.1.9.3
   Software Directive
      implementation of 7.1.4, 7.1.6

Confidential information 1.2, 1.3, 1.5.5,
                                10.1–10.4
   employment cases and 10.3, 10.3.2
   essentials of 10.1, 10.3.1
   history 10.3
   protection
      reasons for 10.2
   public information 10.3, 10.3.1
   remedies 10.4
   skill and experience information 10.3
   trade secrets 10.3
   trivia information 10.3

Copyright 1.1, 1.3, 1.4, 1.5.1,
                  5.1–5.2.3.5, 6.1–6.9
   authorship 5.2.2.2
   cable re-transmission 5.1.2
   copying
      incidental 5.1.5
      meaning of 5.1.5
      transient 5.1.5
      conscious 6.4
      unconscious 6.4
      co-incidence and 6.4
   computer programs
      See Computer programs
   databases
      See Databases
   distribution right 5.2.3.3
   duration of 5.2.2.4
   enforcement provisions 6.2
   future developments and 11.5
   harmonisation of terms of
      protection of 5.1.2
   ideas and 5.2.2
   infringement 5.2.2, 5.2.3, 6.2, 6.3
      dealing with infringing copy 6.6.1
      High Court action 6.7.1.1
      innocent 5.2.3, 6.5
      permitting use of premises for 6.6.2
      primary 6.6
      secondary 6.6
      substantial part of work 6.4
   Information Society 5.1.6
   internet
      exploitation of 5.1.3
   introduction to 5.1, 6.1
   law relating to 5.1.1
      European Community law
         obligations 5.1.2, 5.1.3
      international treaty obligations 5.1.4
      modernising 5.1.5
   lending rights 5.1.2, 5.2.3.4
   licences 9.5.14
      See Intellectual property

making available right	5.1.5, 5.2.3.2, 7.1.8.2, 8.6
meaning of	5.2.1
moral rights	5.1.6
offences	6.8
types of	6.8
originality	5.2.2.1
ownership	5.2.2.3
piracy	5.1.1, 5.1.4
presumption of	6.7.1
remedies	6.7
civil	6.7.1, 6.7.2
order for delivery up	6.7.2.1, 6.7.2.2, 6.7.2.3
order for seizure	6.7.2.1, 6.7.2.3
seizure by copyright owner	6.7.2.4
rental rights	5.1.2, 5.2.3.4, 6.4
reproduction right	5.2.3.1, 7.1.8.1
restricted acts	5.2.3–5.2.3.5
rights management information	5.1.5
satellite broadcasting	5.1.2
search warrants	6.9
seizure	6.9
substantial part of work	6.4
works	
artistic	1.3, 5.1.1, 5.2.2, 5.2.2.1, 5.2.2.4, 7.1.1
broadcast	5.2.2, 5.2.2.4
cable programmes	5.2.2
computer	5.2.2.4
dramatic	1.3, 5.2.2, 5.2.2.1.2, 5.2.2.4
films	5.2.2, 5.2.2.4
musical	1.3, 5.2.2, 5.2.2.1.3, 5.2.2.4
original databases	5.2.2, 5.2.2.4
original literary	5.2.2, 5.2.2.1.1, 7.1.1, 7.1.2, 7.1.4
originality of	5.2.2.1
sound recordings	5.2.2, 5.2.2.4
typographical arrangement of published editions	5.2.2

Databases	5.1.2, 5.1.6
See also Computer programs; Copyright	
definition of	7.2.2
duration of protection	7.2.5
expiry of right of	7.2.5
non-original	7.2.2
original	5.2.2, 5.2.2.4
definition of	7.2.1
original intellectual creation	7.2.1
protection of	7.2–7.3
qualifying for	7.2.3
restricted acts	7.2.4
extraction	7.2.4
re-utilisation	7.2.4
Design	
See Industrial designs	
definition of	8.1, 8.2

Industrial designs	1.3, 1.4, 1.5.2, 8.1–8.22
community design right (CD)	8.4
registered (RCD)	8.4.2
unregistered (UCD)	8.4.1
component parts	8.7
compulsory licences	8.15
definition of	8.1, 8.14
delivery up, tight of	8.19
falsification of register	8.21
filing date	8.11
groundless threats of proceedings	8.18
individual character	8.7
infringement	8.16
interconnections, designs of	8.9
licences	9.3
See also Intellectual property	
making available right	8.6
See also Copyright	
new	
meaning of	8.6
offences	8.20
ownership	8.10
priority right	8.12
product, definition of	8.2
protection of	8.3
registerable	8.5
registration, effect of	8.13
remedies	8.17
seizure, right of	8.19
technical functions	8.9
Intellectual property	
definition of	8.1, 8.2
historical background to	1.5–1.6
International Bureau of the World Intellectual Property Organisation (WIPO)	2.4.3
introduction to	1.1–1.6
licences	9.1–9.64
anatomy of a licence agreement	9.5
competition law issues and	9.3
exclusivity	4.8, 9.3, 9.5.4
key provisions of	9.5
assignability	9.5, 9.5.7
confidentiality	9.5, 9.5.15
See also Confidential information	

consideration provisions	9.5, 9.5.10
description of the licensed IP	9.5, 9.5.2
dispute resolution	9.5, 9.5.18
identity of parties	9.5, 9.5.1
indemnities	9.5, 9.5.13
infringement claims against third parties	9.5, 9.5.14
licensee, obligations of	9.5, 9.5.17
licensor, obligations of	9.5, 9.5.16
ownership of improvements	9.5.11
payment provisions	9.5, 9.5.10
renewal provisions	9.5, 9.5.8
right to sub-contract	9.5, 9.5.6
right to sub-licence	9.5, 9.5.6
scope of exclusivity	9.5, 9.5.4
scope of permitted purpose	9.5, 9.5.3
term of licence	9.5, 9.5.8
termination provisions	9.5, 9.5.9
territorial scope of agreement	9.5, 9.5.5
warranties	9.5, 9.5.12
know-how	9.3, 9.5.8
legislative framework for	9.1.1
meaning of	9.1
mixed patent licences	9.3, 9.5.8
pre-contract considerations	9.4
pure patent licence	9.3
recordal of	9.2
tax	9.6–9.6.4
fees and	9.6.4
stamp duty	9.6.3, 11.6
VAT	9.6.2
withholding	9.6.1
technology transfer block exemption (TTBE)	9.3, 9.5.5, 9.5.11
vertical agreements block exemption	9.3

Internet
See Copyright

Inventions
See Patents

Irish Patent Office	2.4, 2.5, 2.6.1, 2.7
national filing at	2.4.1, 2.4.3
procedure before	2.7
website address of	2.4.1

Passing off	1.3, 1.5.4, 3.1–3.10
See also Trade marks	

business element	3.2, 3.6
character merchandising	3.8
circumstances for case of	3.2–3.9
copycat cases	3.3
core principles	3.2
damage caused by	3.7
definition of	3.2
generally	3.1
goodwill element and	3.2, 3.6, 3.7
look alike cases	3.3
made by trader in course of trade	3.2, 3.4
misrepresentation	3.2, 3.3
personality rights	3.9
practical steps towards dealing with	3.10
prospective customers	3.2, 3.5
Patents	**1.1, 1.3, 1.4, 1.5.3, 4.1–4.16.3**
advantages of	4.4.1
agents	4.15
communications with solicitors	4.16.1
role of in litigation	4.15
amendment	4.12
application for	4.5
claiming priority	4.5.5
Europe in	4.5.6
filing a first Irish	4.5.3
filing a first application elsewhere	4.5.4
international	4.5.7
novelty searches	4.5.1
preparation for	4.5.2
customs and excise	4.16.3
disadvantages of	4.4.1
disclosure, action for	4.16.2
free movement of goods	4.10.2
future developments and	11.4
groundless threats remedy for	4.13
ideas	4.4
infringement	4.7
action for	4.8
defences to	4.10
abuse of position	4.10.2
aircraft and	4.10.10.2
connection	4.10.2
consent of proprietor of patent	4.10.1
continue use before priority date	4.10.5
continue use while patent lapsed	4.10.6
dominant position	4.10.2
Euro	4.10.2
exhaustion of rights	4.10.2

experimental use	4.10.8	types of	4.3.1
extemporaneous preparation		pharmaceuticals	1.3
on prescription	4.10.9	privileged communications	
hovercrafts and	4.10.10.2	solicitors and patent agents	4.16.1
invalid patent	4.10.5	revocation	4.11
not novel	4.10.3	grounds for	4.11
private use	4.10.7	short term	4.1, 4.3.3
restrictive conditions,		supplementary protection	
breach of	4.10.10.3	certificates (SPC)	4.3.4
ships and	4.10.10.1	duration of	4.3.4
staple commercial		granting of	4.3.4
products	4.7.2	duration of	4.3.4
vehicles	4.10.10.2		
direct infringing acts	4.7.1		
indirect	4.7.2	**Trade marks**	**1.1, 1.3, 1.4, 1.5.4,**
knowledge of	4.7		**2.1–2.24.6**
liability for	4.7.2	altering details of	2.15
remedies for	4.9	certification mark	2.20
certificate of contested		collective mark	2.20
validity	4.9	community trade mark (CTM)	2.4, 2.4.2,
costs	4.9, 4.9.5		2.6.2, 2.7, 2.8,
damages and account			2.24, 4.10.2
of profits	4.9, 4.9.1, 4.9.1.1	acquiescence	2.24.5
destruction of	4.9, 4.9.3	duration	2.24.1
injunction	4.9	infringement of	2.24.2, 2.24.4
order for delivery up	4.9, 4.9.3	jurisdiction	2.24.3
short term patents and	4.3.3	remedies	2.24.4
statutory exceptions to	4.10, 4.14	seniority	2.24.6
declaration of non-		Customs Authority	
infringement	4.14	powers of	2.13
international conventions	4.2	definition of	2.2
Community Patent Convention	4.2.4	devices	2.3
European Patent		famous	2.21
Convention	4.2.3, 4.5.6	filing of application	2.5
Paris Convention for Protection		future developments and	11.3
of Industrial Property	4.2.1, 4.5.5	legislation for	2.1
Patent Co-operation		licensing	2.16, 9.3, 9.5.3, 9.5.14
Treaty	4.2.2, 4.5.7	See also Intellectual property	
Know-how	4.4, 4.5	exclusive licences	2.17
advantages of	4.4.1	non-exclusive licences	2.18
disadvantages of	4.4.1	logos	2.3
definition of	4.4	Irish Patents Office	2.4, 2.5
law for	4.1	See Irish Patents Office	
licences	9.5.14	infringing use	2.10, 2.11
See Intellectual property		proceedings	2.13, 2.14
ownership of right to	4.6	reliefs available for	2.13
co-ownership of	4.6.1	what is not	2.12
patentable inventions	4.3.1	invalidity of	2.19, 2.19.3
Europe in	4.5.6	jurisdiction	2.23
inventive step	4.3.2	Madrid Protocol filing	2.4, 2.4.3
meaning of	4.3.1, 4.4	national filing of	2.4.1
novelty	4.5, 4.3.2, 4.5.1	offences	2.22
technical field	4.3.1	Office for Harmonisation in the	
technical problem	4.3.1	Internal Market (OHIM)	2.4, 2.4.2, 2.5

passing off and	1.5.4	places for	2.4
See also Passing off		refusal of	2.6.1–2.6.2
personal property		types for	2.3
recognised as	2.15	revocation of	2.19, 2.19.2
registration of	2.6	rights, limitation of	2.9
dealings with	2.15	selective filing in individual	
duration of	2.8	countries	2.4, 2.4.4
effects of	2.10	surrender of	2.19, 2.19.1
infringement	2.10	transferring of	2.15
international	2.4.3	well-known	2.21
non-use of	2.9	definition of	2.21